Heart4Iran

The Forbidden Stories

DR. MIKE ANSARI

Ordering Information: Please visit Amazon, or our website at http://www.heart4iran.com.

Cover Photo Copyright © Shutterstock
Cover Design Copyright ©

ISBN: 1530665442
ISBN-13: 978-1530665440

DEDICATION

This book is dedicated to all of those dreaming for a better life, hope and happiness.

INDEX

God is at work. Jesus is building His church. The Spirit is transforming lives. The Gospel is on the move. These are not the typical statements that come to your mind when you think about the Islamic Republic of Iran! And yet these are exactly the kinds of statements that describe what is happening every day in the lives of countless Iranians in Iran and around the world. I am deeply grateful for Dr. Mike Ansari sharing with us some of these incredible testimonies of God's grace touching every level of Iranian society. Read these true stories and be encouraged with the Gospel, the power of God that brings salvation to everyone who believes!

-Rev. Sasan Tavassoli, PhD
Iranian Missionary

ACKNOWLEDGMENTS

I cannot say thanks enough for each and every person who courageously shared their story in this book.

I would like to thank all of the staff, employees and volunteers without whom it would have been impossible to be where we are today.

I also would like to thank friends of Heart4Iran and its family of worldwide partnerships for standing in perseverance. Together we are better.

Thanks to my family who has been with me from the beginning.

Thanks to Renee Fisher for helping me craft this book. For her careful attention to detail and joyful spirit for the Iranian people. May God continue to bless your ministry as you spur others forward.

FOREWORD

If I could choose to live at any time in history, I would choose today. Why? Because we are closer today to fulfilling the Great Commission than ever before. One of the toughest, most challenging places to do that is the country of Iran.

Iran has a rich Christian history that dates back to the Day of Pentecost. The first three people groups to respond to the Gospel Peter preached were from Iran. But for hundreds of years, that Good News was lost to them.

When we think about where we should do evangelism, shouldn't we think of those areas of Iran that have less than one out of every 10,000 people who identify as followers of Christ? And if we are thinking about where we want to go to preach the Gospel or where we might send those believers who are inside the country, surely we would want to send them to the places that have been most neglected by traditional mission work.

That is the heart of God. He cared about one lost coin and one lost sheep and one lost son. We ought to be saying of those difficult areas: "Let's go *there!*"

As a church, we have reached a lot of people, but the great failing of the church is that we keep going where we have already been. We keep going to the easy places. In Iran, there are twenty-three different people groups and different territories where the Gospel has not been heard in centuries. We should engage those people and those places.

Iran is more strategic as a nation in the Great Commission than ever before. The nation of Iran contains more than 75 million people who are desperate for hope and change. I thank my colleague, Dr. Mike Ansari, for capturing the evidence of the work of the Holy Spirit that has accompanied the Good News broadcast into those places to those desperate people in *this day*.

I hope these stories inspire you as they have encouraged me. God is at work! Today is the day of the Lord!

Sincerely,
Elizabeth Schenkel
Production Executive/Writer/Strategist, JESUS Film Project

INTRODUCTION

Abbas Milani, Director of Islamic Studies at Stanford University, shared in his TED Talk that Iran does not deserve to be stereotyped.[1] I agree with him. *Why?*

As President of Heart4Iran, my mission and vision is to inspire, engage and transform the nation of Iran for hope and change. At Heart4Iran, ours is not a political platform but a spiritual one.

Despite the popular notion that Iran is a terrorist nation, Iran's young people are bright, savvy, better educated and less religiously zealous compared to the surrounding Arab nations. They are more advanced than any previous generation. There is supporting evidence that Iranian migrants help contribute to the academic and financial infrastructure of the host country.

I know because *I* am one of them.

I was born in Iran, but left for good when I was twelve years old. Unfortunately, I witnessed the death of a lot of young impressionable people, including my cousin, many of whom were seeking change during the early years of Iranian Islamic revolution.

Today, young Iranians still play a key role. In fact, seventy percent of the population of Iran is under thirty years old.[2] They want to be a part of the international community and globalization. Iranian youth are already exposed to global media, ideas and culture through satellite television, social media and the Internet. Forty million Iranians have access to the Internet, including five million of those who have a Facebook account even though it is banned inside the country of Iran.[3]

Despite prohibitions on women's rights, Iranian women account for sixty-five percent of university attendance with a sixty percent graduation rate—higher than men. However, many of Iran's young and educated are unemployed. The vast majority conform to the system and stay quiet while those who dare to ask questions and seek answers feel hopeless and live under the constant threat of detentions, torture, expulsion from universities, and the expanding powers of paramilitary forces.

Although an Islamic nation, culturally and socially most Iranians don't define their spiritual journey in the sole context of Islam. The influence of Zoroastrianism, Mithraism, Sufism, mysticism, etc., has turned Iran into a cradle for higher conscious and subconscious pursuit. Despite Islam's constant presence in their social and cultural fabric, many Iranians believe religion limits their true spirituality and labels their esoteric experiences as heresy and as occult. For example, after the Islamic Revolution of 1979, people began asking some simple yet profound questions like:

How does this faith and belief define my relationship with my creator or my values as an individual in society? As a family unit? As a member in a larger global community?

The pre-scripted answers given to these *forbidden* questions have left the majority unsatisfied. They want to discover *who* they are outside of the religious identity bestowed upon them by the system.

Millions of Iranians are hungry for hope and change and are questioning traditional forms of authority. Iran is now, more than ever, proving to be a blueprint for the failure of Islam. Because the strict authoritarian regime limits and forbids young people from finding the freedom they so crave, Islam's credibility is decreasing rapidly while creating a generation of spiritually-hungry Iranians.

Iranians are affectionate and love to love. Iranians are also hungry for love. This innate desire is forcefully hidden under the veil of darkness covering them in the name of God. Many are therefore attracted to the simple message of Jesus: God is love. This has led to a historic and organic growth of Christianity inside Iran, evidenced by one of the fastest growing underground church movements in the world![4]

To meet their demand, Heart4Iran's media arm, Mohabat TV, along with its family of partners, has been broadcasting Farsi Christian programming into Iran, Afghanistan and Tajikistan since 2006. The following stories are original accounts of people who have engaged us with their story. Depending on your beliefs or theology, some of these stories may be difficult to believe, yet these individuals know them to be true. To retain the character of the original text, we have chosen not to heavily edit these testimonies. As you read, you will be inspired to see a new wave of enlightenment through the scope of Christianity.

1: RESTORING THE BROKEN

"Blessed are the *poor in spirit*: for theirs is the kingdom of heaven" (Matthew 5:3, emphasis added).

Parisa used to be a believer until she married a fanatic Muslim. She thought she could convert him. She eventually gave up. After a usual doctor's check up, she found out that she had a big tumor and couldn't get pregnant. Devastated, she cried to Jesus and called the counseling center at Mohabat TV for prayer. She confessed that she had sinned and asked God for forgiveness and restoration with her husband. The counselors prayed for her, but she wasn't healed. Parisa had to have an operation which would prevent her from ever getting pregnant. On the day of the operation, she had her last ultrasound. Stunned, the doctor said she did *not* need an operation! The tumor was gone. God did a miracle, and she is completely healed!

2: Mohammad called from the United States asking for prayer for his son who had cancer in his lymph nodes. His son had a bone marrow transplant and several other operations but none helped. The doctors had given up on him. After Mohammad prayed with the counselors, Jesus healed his son *completely*!

3: Zohreh prayed with a host during a live Mohabat TV program. She accepted Jesus as her Savior and asked for prayer for her painful disk complication. She was instantly healed and rejoiced! The pain was *gone*.

4: While changing channels, a couple came across a live Mohabat TV program that was praying for people's needs.

They called in to ask for prayer for their son, who was in a bad accident. He was paralyzed from the neck down. During the prayer, their son was able to blink his eyes and subsequently accepted Jesus in his heart along with the rest of his family.

5: Mansour liked watching Mohabat TV but was never a Christian. He was not interested until he became *very* sick. While he was laying in bed, he remembered hearing that Jesus is God and is able to heal! He prayed: "Lord Jesus if you are truly God, you can heal me. If you do, I will become a Christian, go to church and tell everyone that you are the God who heals!" That very moment, Mansour felt a plastic-like covering from his head to his toes fall off his body. He was healed instantly! He emailed Mohabat TV to share his prayer and to thank us for the programs.

6: Farzad became a Christian after watching one of the testimonies on Mohabat TV. His daughter was very sick with kidney failure, and after he prayed for her, she was completely healed. His wife was against Christianity. After she saw their daughter healed, and noticed a change in her husband, she accepted Christ as her Savior. Farzad said God has answered *all* of his prayers ever since, and his relationship with his wife is better than ever—even after twenty plus years of marriage.

7: Maryam's son was born with a stomach deformity. They didn't have money to operate until he was four years old. After the operation, he would not come back to consciousness. The doctors told Maryam to pray. She was a Muslim and only knew to pray in Islam. While sitting in the hospital lobby, a woman approached her and asked how she could pray for her. She explained her son's situation, and the women told her about Jesus. The lady explained that Jesus can and *will* heal her son. She prayed and left. After a couple hours her son came out of the operating room and recovered quickly. The doctors said it was a miracle! She knew it was

Jesus who healed her son. Ever since, she has looked for that woman or any Christian who could tell her more about this Jesus. She was told about Mohabat TV through a friend of a friend. She called to tell us about her son and that she had been looking for Jesus. Excited to learn more, Maryam prayed for salvation.

8: Marzieh called from Holland and asked us to pray that God would heal her of cancer. She had seen on Mohabat TV that we pray for the sick on live shows. The counselors prayed and told her about Christianity and salvation in Jesus. Marzieh said she wanted to feel better—then she would make a decision to become a Christian or not. The next week she went to the doctor for a checkup and to be scheduled for chemotherapy. When the doctor checked, he didn't find any trace of cancer cells. She no longer needed further treatment. She realized that Jesus had healed her! She called and *confessed* with the Mohabat counselors that Jesus Christ is truly the Son of God.

9: Javad went to Turkey for a doctor visit. He was told this doctor could help him with his disease. While he was there, a tourist gave him a Persian Gospel to read. Javad took it back to Iran, but didn't pay much attention until he came across Mohabat TV. When he heard them reading from a book called the "Gospel" he remembered that he had the *same* book. He started to read it, and called our counseling center to give his life to the Author of the book! Javad said that Jesus healed him from his disease.

10: Zahra had a tumor on her back next to her spine. The doctors said nothing could be done. Even if they operated she would have to be in a wheelchair the rest of her life. She called in for prayer from Iran. Within weeks, she started feeling better and had *no* pain. She went back to the doctor, and he said it was a miracle! How could a huge tumor just vanish? Only God could do that! She accepted Jesus as her

Lord and is so healthy now that she actually goes bike riding! 11: Ebrahim, a Muslim, called in for prayer for his eight-year-old daughter who had leukemia. The counselors explained the Gospel, and he trusted the Lord. He called back four months later and gave his testimony during a live show that Jesus healed his daughter. He said *all* the doctors were surprised and couldn't explain this miracle. Ebrahim thanked Mohabat's prayer team.

12: Roudabeh, an old lady who was uneducated, called for prayer. She opened her heart for the Lord when she heard the Gospel. The counselors sent her a New Testament upon her request. Roudabeh was illiterate and only able to write her name, but she trusted in the Lord. After she prayed, she was able to *read* the Gospel. Her husband says this can only be a miracle that she is able to read!

13: Hossein called from Boushehr asking for prayer. His wife left him and took their six-year-old son. He cried night and day for them to return. One night he came across Mohabat TV. He called to pray with a counselor and gave his life to Jesus. After two days, Hossein called back to say that Jesus gave him so much peace. He had mental problems and used to take pills, but he said he is so happy that he doesn't take them anymore because Jesus healed him *completely*. He believes his wife and son will return because Jesus answers prayers!

14: Sara called during a live Mohabat TV show for her friend Shima who was still bleeding after giving birth to her baby. The next day after she received prayer, the bleeding *stopped*.

15: Sassan called Mohabat TV to share his testimony. He shared about his salvation and the healing power of Jesus. He had stomach cancer, couldn't eat and was very weak. But in the name of Jesus, Sassan is healed and cancer free now.

16: Roghayeh had headaches for twenty years. She went to the doctors and used all kinds of chemical and herbal medicines, but none helped. One day she watched Mohabat TV and called in for prayer. The counselors prayed for her, and she never had the headaches anymore. Roghayeh was completely healed! She was very thankful and called back and prayed to receive Christ as her Lord and Savior.

17: Omid's brother had no hope, according to a doctor's report. They said he would *die*. Omid called Mohabat TV for prayer, and after praying for his brother, he became well. The doctor said that his brother would die, but the Lord healed him.

18: Farkhondeh asked for prayer for her mother who needed surgery for her osteoporosis. The doctors didn't want to do the surgery because her mother had other problems as well. Farkhondeh had *faith* and prayed with a counselor. One of the doctors decided to do the surgery, and now her mother is well.

19: Rahmat was in a car accident when the driver dosed and veered off the road. He was sitting in front passenger seat and tried to control the steering wheel. He was thrown from the car and hit his head hard. At the hospital, the doctors said he would be paralyzed. He had given his heart to the Lord two weeks before, so he prayed and asked Jesus to heal him. When he called Mohabat TV, he couldn't speak well or control his tongue movement. Rahmat said, "Jesus healed me!" He was crying and said God loved him so much and he even testified to the doctors, "The God who created me, healed me!" While in the hospital, he visited his mother who had a heart attack days before. He prayed for his mother also, and she was *healed*. They were released from the hospital together!

20: A woman called for prayer for healing. An unknown virus had entered her body. She needed chemotherapy. While she was talking with Mohabat counselors, they realized she was not born again. They explained how to give your heart and life completely to Jesus. The woman cried and prayed. She called the next day from the hospital in complete peace. She said, "Since we prayed I am so light and blessed and happy." She told the counselors that she didn't like her hospital room, so she prayed, and the Lord *answered*. The hospital changed her room. She asked the counselors to keep her in their prayers for healing, knowing that God is with her.

21: Nina had cancer. She called to pray for healing. The counselors prayed for her salvation, too, and she was full of peace. They kept in touch and encouraged her daily. Finally, she went to hospital for treatment, because she wasn't feeling good. After chemotherapy, Nina got much worse. She called us crying to say that there was no *hope* for her. Her checkup showed that she needed more chemotherapy. The counselors prayed and encouraged her to trust in the Lord. The next day she called, "I can't believe it! I am healed!" She went to the hospital for chemotherapy. The doctors never do a checkup, but for some reason they wanted to check her before giving her the treatment. She agreed. They didn't find any trace of cancer.

22: Nasrin had a brain tumor. While at the hospital, a lady told her to watch Mohabat TV. She called and asked what the programs were about. The counselors explained how salvation is through Jesus alone. She prayed to receive Christ with her husband after she got home from the hospital. The counselors continue to pray for her healing.

23: Dooman was healed of prostate cancer. He called from Iran and gave his testimony on air. He said he prayed and asked Jesus, "Who is this God Almighty, to heal me?" He went back for a check up, and the doctors couldn't find any cancer cells! Jesus *healed* him of his cancer.

24: Mansour called from London and testified during a live Mohabat TV show that he has been healed of blindness. He was seventy-seven years old and completely blind in one eye. He could only see thirty percent in the other eye. The counselors prayed for him, and he was healed. Mansour didn't *expect* to be healed. He said he only accepted the prayer to be nice and polite. When he realized what just happened, he said he couldn't wait to testify to everyone about it.

25: Pari from Iran called to give her testimony. She had a tumor in her head and could not walk. After asking Jesus for healing, she felt better and went to the doctor and insisted on another checkup. The doctors were shocked that she was completely healed. They asked her what happened. She proclaimed that the Lord Jesus Christ healed her. Soon the word spread in the hospital, and *everyone* was praising the Lord with Pari!

26: A man had been a Christian for a few weeks and saw many miracles. One night his wife told him that since he believes in God so much, why doesn't he pray that God would heal her eyes? She had pain in her eyes for quite a while. He stood in the middle of the room, looked up to heaven and prayed, "Lord, you are God. You can heal my wife and take the pain away completely. Please heal her." She was *healed*. He called Mohabat TV to give his testimony of his wife's miracle healing!

27: Naser called from Russia accidentally. He was changing channels and intended to call another channel. He had cancer and was in the hospital. The counselors explained the Good News, and he prayed for salvation. They prayed and believed for his healing. Naser was very *happy* that he called Mohabat TV.

28: Mohammad watched Mohabat TV and called to give his

life to Jesus. Jesus changed his life and gave him indescribable peace. Later, he had an accident and was in a coma for a few months. God healed Mohammad from his coma, and because of that *all* his family gave their lives to Jesus. He called to share with everyone about his miracles.

29: Mojgan asked for prayer for her mom who was in a coma for two years. While talking with the counselors, she gave her heart to Jesus. Mojgan has peace now. She says God has *changed* her life. In spite of her mom's situation, she says she has peace in her life.

30: Akbar, a university professor and author, used to practice meditation because he was depressed from childhood. He came across Mohabat TV and started watching. One day he prayed for salvation during one of the shows. He called to tell us that his depression left him *instantly*. He also had severe back pain, and God healed it as well. His life, he said, was changed completely.

31: Ali called from Iran to ask for prayer. He couldn't sleep. He prayed with the counselors. He called back the next day to say that he slept all night for the *first* time. Then, Ali accepted Jesus as his Lord.

32: Maryam had problems in her marriage. They were on the verge of divorce. One night, watching Mohabat TV, she gave her heart to the Lord and was saved. She told her husband, and he believed in his heart, too. They have a daughter who had bone cancer. They prayed to all the prophets and took her everywhere for healing, but when they prayed to Jesus she was healed *completely*. They shared that they are in awe of God's goodness to them daily.

33: Abutaleb gave his life to the Lord during a Mohabat TV show. He called to say he was witnessing to everyone and wanted us to pray for them to be saved. When he prays for the sick, they *all* get healed. Abutaleb is happy that God is using him to bless many.

34: Rana asked for prayer for her son who was sick. The counselors prayed, and she saw Jesus in a light come into her room, visit her and *assure* her that her son would be well. She said Jesus healed her son!

35: Maryam said when she watched Mohabat TV, her eyes started itching. A white fog that bothered one of her eyes for months became stronger. She called for prayer, and after the host prayed for healing, she felt she could see clearly. Maryam went to the doctor who was surprised that the same *weak* eye was completely healed! She told him that Jesus healed her.

36: Masoomeh called Mohabat TV and testified on air that Jesus healed her knee pain after years of suffering. She was *sixty* years old when she gave her life to Jesus.

37: Hajar requested prayer for healing. Her doctors said it might be bone cancer, and she needed an MRI. She was very concerned and asked the counselors to pray for good results. Hajar called a few days later to testify on a live show that God gave her *good* health. There was no more cancer.

38: A man called Mohabat TV, wishing to remain anonymous. He asked for prayer for his wife who had a skin problem for seventy-five years. He called back to share that his wife was *completely* healed in Jesus' name.

39: Soheila called from Germany with bad leg pain. The counselors prayed for her, and she was healed. Soheila testified that the Lord took away *all* of the pain and freed her.

40: Kamil called from Iran asking us to pray for his brother who was in a mental hospital. He was often forgetful. The counselors prayed, and Kamil's brother was healed *and* released from the mental hospital. He called back to say thanks and received Jesus as his Savior.

41: Mohammad called from Shiraz, Iran, to say he had knee pain and needed surgery. One day on Mohabat TV, the host prayed live for his healing. Mohammad called to testify that he received healing and was pain *free*. The doctors confirmed he no longer needed surgery.

42: Fariba from Iran watched Mohabat TV for more than a year and became a Christian through the shows. When her aunt got breast cancer, she called for prayer. For the first time in her life, Fariba confessed that she had accepted Jesus. It had been a secret in her heart because of her *fear* of Muslims. Her aunt was healed completely of cancer and accepted Christ as her Savior by praying with Fariba.

43: Khadijeh called Mohabat TV desperate for prayer for her sister who about to undergo a major surgery on her heart. The counselors prayed with her. Khadijeh called back the next week and testified on live show that her sister was *completely* healed.

44: Alireza called from Iran. He said he had a lot of back pain. The doctors advised him to have an operation, which he couldn't afford. The counselors prayed for him, and Alireza was completely healed!

45: Fereshteh called from Ahwaz, Iran. She didn't have a good relationship with her husband. Since she got married, she couldn't get pregnant. She watched Mohabat TV and heard the host saying, "Sometimes you have to fast and ask Jesus for your miracle." She prayed to Jesus for the first time saying, "Jesus please give me a baby. Prove yourself as God and I will believe in you, and I will fast for three days." She fasted and waited in faith for Jesus to answer her prayers. She called Mohabat TV weeks later to say she was pregnant and wanted to become a Christian.

46: Habib, an Afghan, called from Sweden. He shared that about sixteen years ago the Taliban harmed his eyes. He was climbing the roof of his house to fix it when he accidentally had eye contact with his neighbor's wife and daughter who were sitting in their yard. They immediately covered their faces and rushed back into their house. He said had no intention of intruding in their home. Two hours later, the Taliban arrived. They dragged him, beat him and imprisoned him. After a few days, they took him to a small assembly where there was a mullah. His neighbor was there, too. The mullah said his neighbor complained about him looking into their privacy. In this case, the mullah said Habib had committed adultery with his eyes. As a warning they put fire in his eyes. Because of that, one of his eyes is blind and he can barely see through the other. His shared that his neighbor was not satisfied with the punishment. They said it wasn't enough. They demanded that he must be put to death. Habib feared for his life and ran away to Iran where he asked a doctor to help him with his eyes. The doctors in Iran said they couldn't do anything, and he fled further to Turkey and Greece. He desperately ended up in Sweden. For a year and a half, the doctors in Sweden tried very hard to help Habib, but they also said they may *not* be able to help. At this point, Habib said he was hopeless and wanted to commit suicide. He couldn't because he remembered his children back home in Afghanistan. In his hopelessness, a new friend came to him and said, "There is one way you have not yet tried." Habib said he answered him, saying, "Look, I have always prayed, fasted and visited the Islamic saints' tombs. I wept, and I think there are no other ways for my wounds and sorrows." His friend replied, "No there is one more way, and if you do not become angry at me, I will tell you about that way. You need to knock at the door of the house of Jesus Christ. I have faith that He will help you." When Habib heard this, it was like a new *hope* in his heart. He said he found Mohabat TV through the Internet. He heard the miracles Jesus performed in healing people. He moved to find a Persian church in another city. He told the people in the church how he found Jesus and asked for prayer for his eyes. He said everyone in that church hugged him, welcomed him and answered all his questions. Habib met a fellow Afghan who had been a Christian for two years and asked him about the change in his life. He said, "I cannot describe the joy I have in Christ." That was the night Habib trusted in Jesus fully and was later baptized. The church continued to pray for the healing of his eyes. Amazingly, soon after he trusted Jesus, the doctors who said they could not help reopened his case. Habib said his joy is not to be healed physically anymore, but if he is he will continue to praise the Lord! His true joy is that he found God.

47: Zahra called from Iran to ask for prayer for her and her family. Her mother and her sister suffered from rheumatism, and she had a hearing problem. Her left ear was sensitive to sounds, and it bothered her *all* the time. She said one of her sisters had OCT and was depressed. She prayed for salvation. She trusts that God will heal her and her family.

48: A woman's son was diagnosed with MS in his last year of high school, about five years ago. She said her heart broke when she heard he had MS. She hated everything, including her family and even God. She asked God, "Why did you give me a son? Don't you care about my pain? Why are You sitting in heaven and doing nothing?" She was disappointed and found herself in darkness. After a while, she met Jesus Christ. Through many tears, she understood that He came down, dwelt in a body and died on the cross. He also had pain and was wounded. The woman said when she heard *this* message, she thought she wanted this God because He feels her pain. She became a Christian, but it wasn't easy and she doubted a lot. Anytime she worried, God told her not to worry. "Come unto me, all ye that labor and are heavy laden and I will give you rest" (Matthew 11:28). God gave her peace. She called Mohabat TV to share that a new MRI revealed that her son was healed of MS!

49: Parvin called to share that she couldn't sleep because her toes were in too much pain from diabetes. She asked God to help her. After a half an hour, her pain was going away. This continued every night until Parvin called to ask for prayer. She said her pain was gone, and she *praises* the Lord because He is Almighty. "Glory to the name of Jesus that healed my feet. My doctor said because I am diabetic, my vessels get clogged, and there is nothing he can do. Nothing. But I got healed without any medicine."

50: A woman got saved after her daughter called Mohabat TV about four years ago. She had lost a son who was only twenty-two years old. Her daughter suffered from depression because of this and was at a dead end in her life. Years later, the daughter has led more than ten family members to the Lord. She called back for prayer for a friend who needed surgery for a larger stone in his gallbladder and was in severe pain. After receiving prayer, the friend went to his doctor for check up and ultrasound. No stone was found, and the doctors cancelled the surgery!

51: A woman called Mohabat TV saying she couldn't breathe. She felt something heavy on her chest. She wanted to call her husband to be admitted to the hospital and see a cardiologist. She couldn't even take a glass of water into her hands, but after receiving prayer for healing in the powerful name of Jesus', she said the pain was gone. She could breath. The heaviness was gone! She was asked to get up and pour a glass of water for herself, and when she did, she said, "This is a miracle." *Immediately*, she accepted Jesus as her Lord and Savior!

52: Mehdi called Mohabat TV and was so much in fear

because a doctor recently diagnosed him with AIDS. The program that day was about the blood of Jesus. He called to ask many questions and ended up receiving Jesus as his Lord and Savior. For the next few weeks, he called to ask for continued prayer. "I want to stay alive. Keep me in your prayers, even at church." The counselors told him to begin thanking Jesus for his healing and check back with his doctor. Mehdi did and called us back a week later to testify that the doctor redid the tests. He said, "A miracle has happened." There was no trace of *AIDS* in his blood. Because of this miracle, Mehdi's sisters called Mohabat TV and were saved. All of them are now watching the programs to grow in their new faith.

53: A woman called for prayer because she was in severe pain due to MS and broken legs. The counselors prayed for her healing. After three years of suffering, she got up *without* pain. The woman cried out of joy. She still couldn't put one of her legs on the floor, and in the middle of prayers for her healing, she said "something" came upon her bones. She began to praise Jesus as His healing power was coming upon her and healed her!

54: Mina watched Mohabat TV all the time and wanted to become a Christian, but her husband was strongly against it. She secretly continued to watch anyway! When Mina's husband was taken to prison for fraud, she called the counselors. She prayed to receive Christ as her Lord and Savior. They got her a Bible, and she started reading right away. Mina's husband was miraculously released from prison and saw a change in his wife. He changed his mind, and let her watch Mohabat TV. He didn't want to become a Christian himself, but he asked the counselors to pray for them so they could have children after many years of being barren. Jesus answered their prayers, and Mina called to say she is pregnant!
55: A Hajji (a Muslim who goes to Mecca for pilgrimage)

woman was in the last stage of breast cancer and infection of lungs. Almost unable to breathe, she called in for prayer. The Mohabat TV counselors explained to her about the plan of salvation, and she received Jesus as her Lord and Savior. After receiving prayer for healing, she was able to breathe much better. The woman thanked Jesus.

56: Hossein was a new believer, but he never read the Bible. He only watched Mohabat TV. One day he was so depressed with the pressures he was facing in life that he was walked aimlessly in the streets. Then, he saw a young man carrying a small six-year-old girl. Hossein felt God telling him to go and pray for the girl. He had never prayed in his life other than repeating the salvation prayer. He approached the young man and asked if he could pray for the girl. He laid his hand on the girl's forehead and prayed a simple prayer, "Jesus would you heal her?" Immediately, she opened her eyes. Seeing the miracle, Hossein was empowered by the Holy Spirit to continue praying for the father and his own problems right there on the street. He said *that* night was actually the day he became born again!

57: Maryam had a bent back since birth. Her dad also had the same bent shape in his back. Her mother called the counselors to say that she was ashamed of the attitudes of some of her daughter's classmates. Her daughter had difficulties and struggled with self-esteem. The counselors told them about the woman who had an infirmity for eighteen years, and asked the daughter if she believed Jesus could heal her. She replied, "Yes." She was fifteen when she accepted Jesus as her Savior. Before the eyes of heaven and her mother, when the counselors prayed, the Great Physician touched the daughter's back. They could hear her and her mother's cries of joy. The Lord Jesus healed her instantly and her back was *straightened.*

2: REMOVING THE VEIL OF CAPTIVITY

"Blessed are they that *mourn*: for they shall be comforted" (Matthew 5:4, emphasis added).

58: Fereshteh used to hear sounds and see dark shadows around her. She was always in fear. She went to an Islamic clerk for prayer. He wrote down a prayer for her that she had to have with her all the time. It didn't help. She went to a doctor who said there was no hope for her. Go and kill yourself! One night, Fereshteh was fearful and could not sleep. She prayed that God would end her life. That night, she came across Mohabat TV. She watched for a couple hours straight. When Fereshteh tried to change the channel or turn off the TV, she couldn't so she called the number on the screen to ask for help. She prayed to accept Jesus as her Lord and Savior, and suddenly the sounds *stopped*! She turned off the lights, and there were no longer any dark shadows around her. She was free! She called back the next day to give her testimony on the live show that Jesus gave her peace and her life back.

59: Mahboubeh had a son who was depressed. She called the counselors for prayer, and her son was able to stop taking his medication for depression. When Mahboubeh saw her son was healed completely, she wanted to know about *this* Jesus. She prayed for salvation with the counselors.

60: Zeynab was ready to commit suicide. She had planned everything for a certain night. While she was waiting, she flipped through the channels and came across Mohabat TV. She listened to the host who proclaimed that Jesus came to give life and life abundantly. Zeynab decided to call. She didn't know the show was a repeat and spoke with the counselors who directed her to pray for salvation and receive Jesus as her Lord and Savior. She changed her *suicidal* thoughts and received abundant life in Jesus!

61: Ramin heard about Jesus through his friends but ignored them. One night, he was so depressed that he decided to commit suicide. While contemplating suicide, he flipped through channels and came across Mohabat TV. He called to know more about this Jesus. After a long conversation with our counselors, Ramin gave his *life* to Jesus and was filled with His joy!

62: Hossein wanted to end his life. He was so depressed and tried everything under the sun. He finally he gave up on life. While he was thinking about his suicide, he came across Mohabat TV and started watching for a couple nights until he called the counselors for prayer and to give his life to Jesus! He instantly was filled with peace. The counselors sent Hossein the Bible and followed up with him. He had *many* questions. He was so happy that he met Jesus. He said, "Life has a different meaning now. I am enjoying every minute of it. I hope it never ends!"

63: Arezoo, a middle-aged woman with teenage kids, worked as a cleaning lady. She had many financial problems. She watched Mohabat TV for a while and liked what they said about Jesus. Her problems were so much, and she was so depressed that she forgot about Jesus until one day she was cleaning a house. She was tired of life and thinking of committing suicide when a mighty wind gushed into the room. The voice told her to call Mohabat TV. While still shaking from the encounter, she called to talk with the counselors and prayed to receive Christ as her Lord and Savior!

64: Elizabeth called from England. She was so depressed because the doctors said she might have cancer. She also had problems with her immigration status. The counselors prayed for her through many phone calls and encouraged her to trust God. She called after few days testifying to her miracle. Not only could the doctors *not* find any trace of cancer, but her paperwork was approved the next day!

65: The Mohabat TV counselors accidentally called Masoud from Denmark while trying to connect with a caller in Iran. They started talking with him and explained salvation. He accepted Jesus and was so happy. Masoud explained later that our call was not an accident. He said he felt so depressed and had a lot of problems. Praying with the counselors changed everything for him. He called back five weeks later in a shaky voice and said, "I want to commit suicide and suddenly found your channel. I told myself it is better to call you so you can pray for me as I got the pills ready. I am near my wife and two children who are now sleeping." The counselors assured Masoud that Jesus loved him. It was not an accident that they called him that night five weeks ago or that he came upon the program on this night. They told him as long as his heart was beating, there was hope for him. His children needed their daddy. He was desperate but still listening. He took a deep breath and prayed the prayer of salvation with the counselors. The spirit of death and darkness were removed from him. He said he felt better. He said, "I don't have any more sin? All my sin has been forgiven?" The counselors affirmed that he became God's righteousness in Christ Jesus. He said he was *speechless*. He felt calm because Jesus touched his heart. A few days later, he called back to let the counselors know he led his best friend and his sister, whose husband was a "Basiji," (Iranian Islamic guard) to the Lord.

66: Neda was very depressed and tried to commit suicide many times. Something in her heart told her to go to church. She went and felt peace. She came home to find her maid looking depressed. Neda said if she went to church, she would find peace. Next Sunday, her maid went to church, but Neda forgot to tell her that she was praying for her. On Monday, the maid came and told Neda that she went to church and was so blessed, and a lady named Klara said Jesus told her that God heard Neda's prayer and she shouldn't worry. He would *answer* her prayers. Neda called Mohabat TV to ask our counselors if she could receive the Holy Spirit too. She prayed the salvation prayer and received the Holy Spirit.

67: Sara emailed the Mohabat TV counselors, asking them to guide her on becoming a Christian. While they were responding, Sara called. She said she was in such a hurry. She felt so restless and depressed that she *had* to call. The counselors guided her through a prayer to receive Jesus and to follow Him. Before she hung up the phone, she was so full of joy!

68: A prostitute from Dubai called Mohabat TV. She told the counselors that she was depressed and sick of her life of prostitution. The counselors prayed with her, and she gave her heart to the Lord.

69: Leyla was depressed. She called the Mohabat TV counselors for comfort. She said she sold her body for money. She was sick of prostitution! They shared with her about the love of Jesus and that she should trust him for her needs. She accepted Jesus and immediately felt the peace of the Lord *all* over her.

70: Ali was saved from depression and despair. He called from a village outskirt in Iran. He said he was suffering from severe depression and asked the Mohabat TV counselors for prayer. When they prayed, Ali started crying. He said, "I feel Jesus at my side. He is real!" Even though Ali is uneducated, he started to read the Bible. He wants to know Jesus more.

71: Mohtaram, a young lady from Iran, called the counselors at Mohabat TV to ask for prayer. She was very depressed when she first heard about Christianity. The *moment* the counselors prayed, Mohtaram was filled with peace. She started crying and said she was filled with joy. She gave her heart to Jesus that instant.

72: One of the Mohabat TV shows was talking about forgiveness when Mohammad called. He said he had already tried to commit suicide several times. He asked if God would forgive his sins. The counselors explained that Jesus gave His life to *forgive* us. Mohammad accepted Jesus while sobbing and said he felt his burdens lifting off of him.

73: Fereydoon, a young man from Iran called Mohabat TV. He has a wife and child. He said his family was poor and lived in a crowded place. He worked with welding machines in an industrial company until one day he cut off his arm. He had to stay home and couldn't work. His wife started working, and it really upset him. He never wanted his wife to support him. It hurt his pride, and he fell into a deep depression. Fereydoon committed suicide to end his life because he didn't want to live with one arm. He cut up the veins in his other arm, but he didn't die. God kept him. While he was home doing nothing, he started watching Mohabat TV and came across Joyce Meyers. He watched everyday, twice a day, and gradually his perspective changed. Joyce Meyer's teachings had such a powerful impact on his life that his depression *left!* His attitude change toward his wife and kid. He found an overnight taxi job. He tells all his passengers about Mohabat TV and Joyce Meyer's programs. He called to tell us that he never misses a show. He is actually learning English so he can watch all her teachings. He hopes one day to meet her and talk to her in English. He prayed to receive Jesus and was so happy.

74: Amir's father and brother committed suicide. He wanted to kill himself, too. He was watching Mohabat TV and called the counselors to ask for prayer. They prayed and talked to him about Jesus and His salvation. They explained that Amir didn't need to end his life. He prayed and was filled with *peace*.

75: Ali called from Shiraz, Iran, and was anxious to know about Jesus. After hearing the truth, he prayed to receive Jesus as His Lord and Savior. He used to be very angry, but God changed his life. He was filled with so much peace that he doesn't take his depression pills anymore. He now tells everyone about Jesus!

76: Mahdieh from Kerman, Iran, called Mohabat TV to ask for prayer. She was very depressed. She was so sick of herself and her two unsuccessful marriages that she wanted to end her life. The counselors explained Jesus and His peace. Mahdieh prayed to receive Christ. She was so happy and was filled with peace.

77: Ahmad from Afghanistan was living in Germany. He called Mohabat TV because he had many questions about Christianity. He felt the peace of Jesus as the counselors prayed for him. He accepted Jesus as his Savior. He was fed up of his life and wanted to end it but watching the Mohabat TV channel gave him hope. He was so happy that he called and became a Christian!

78: Shahram from Ardabil, Iran, called Mohabat TV and said he was thinking of committing suicide when he "accidentally" turned on the Mohabat TV channel. He called and prayed to receive Jesus as his Lord and Savior and was filled with joy. Shahram said his wife was against his new faith and wouldn't let him watch Mohabat TV anymore. Two months later, he now he has his own business and is full of joy. He called to say the Lord made such a *change* in his life. Shahram said, "Jesus sent you as an angel to rescue me."

79: Afshin from Afghanistan called Mohabat TV with many questions about Jesus. After a while, he opened up and confessed that he hated himself and was thinking of committing suicide. The counselors asked him to give God one more chance. Afshin prayed to receive Christ as His Lord. He called the next day to say that Jesus lifted *all* his burdens. He felt so light and blessed. For the first time in his life, he said, "I feel joy. I am happy!"

80: Alireza called from Tehran, Iran, with mental problems. He was depressed. He went to every shrine and Imams but received no help. He decided to pray to Jesus and called Mohabat TV. His said his problems were *solved*, and he was now completely fine and happy.

81: A young woman who used to practice divination called Mohabat TV. She said she had been a Christian for three years. She used to take depression medicine to find peace, but nothing worked. Then she believed in Jesus and let Him enter her heart. That same night she threw away *all* her pills. Also that same night, the peace of Jesus entered her heart from that moment on. Three years later, she feels transformed. The young woman said she used to be so nervous. She didn't have a good attitude toward her mother and father and didn't receive any love from them. Now, she is loving them because God *loves* her. She says she still has many problems, but she hopes the youth of Iran will hear her story because God is helping her stay clean from the many temptations of TV, the outside world and different friends.

82: Ahmad called to ask for prayer because he felt abandoned, and his son was in jail. Ahmad prayed and asked Jesus to enter his life with the counselors at Mohabat TV.

83: Hamed was about to commit suicide when he "accidentally" turned on Mohabat TV. In tears, he called the counselors and asked Jesus to come into his heart and help him. He had two children, a two-year-old and a three-year-old, and had many problems. Two days later, he called back to say the Lord delivered him from the spirit of death and suicide. He said his wife, who is a dedicated Muslim, fought with him since he got saved. During Ashoura, a mourning time for Shiite Muslims, instead of going into the streets wearing all black and cutting himself with knives and chains, he rejoiced. Hamed said, "I am like a bird. I want to fly full of joy. My attitude and perspective toward other people has been changed since I prayed two days ago when I gave my heart to Jesus." He said he spoke with his sister, whose husband is a "Pasdar" (Iranian government revolutionary guard), and a friend about Jesus. He told them he was a *changed* man and no longer wanted to commit suicide.

84: An Afghan man living in Iran called Mohabat TV. He said he used to torture and behead women in Afghanistan. He said he was fed up with his life and wanted to know Jesus. The counselors prayed for him, and he accepted the Lord Jesus. He said he felt happiness in his *heart*.

85: Hava got married when she was eleven years old. At the age of eighteen, she got divorced. Years later, she now has an eleven year old son. She has never felt happy in her life, and a darkness always follows her. Hava went to fortune tellers who gave her written prayers that did not help. She wanted to commit suicide, but because of her son she couldn't. Hava started sending her son to Quran classes and asked him to pray for her. One night her son said, "Praying to Allah doesn't work. You should call Mohabat TV. God hears their prayers." She called and asked if there was hope for her. The counselors prayed, and she felt a peace that was so *comforting*! The darkness left immediately.

86: Amir was deep in sin. He was so depressed that he thought of committing suicide when he came across Mohabat TV. He called but didn't know why! He slowly started talking about his intention of killing himself. When Amir heard about the love of Jesus and His forgiveness on the cross, he knew God had other plans. Instead of committing suicide, he *committed* his life to Jesus!

DR. MIKE ANSARI

3: ESCAPING ADDICTION

"Blessed are the *meek*: for they shall inherit the earth"
(Matthew 5:5, emphasis added).

87. Samareh called the Mohabat TV counselors crying that her husband was a drug addict. She asked them to pray for him. They did. That night or the next night, her husband didn't come home. Samareh was upset. She said God never heard her prayers and never would. The next night, her husband came home with flowers and pastries. He claimed he was away at a clinic, changing his blood. He was now clear of drugs. She called back in tears and said, "God answered my prayers. He is so good." *That* night, Samareh's husband called to give his heart to Jesus. The counselors prayed with him, and he was full of the joy of the Lord!

88: Masoumeh, a drug addict, tried everything to overcome her addiction. She called the counselors for prayer because she was pregnant and worried about her baby's health. They prayed for her and the baby. In the last month of her pregnancy, Jesus *freed* her from drugs completely. The baby was born normal. Masoumeh was so thankful.

89: Ardeshir called Mohabat TV on a Monday during a live show. He asked for prayer for his drug addiction. The host prayed for him and led him to salvation. The counselors followed up with him a few weeks later, and Ardeshir's voice was so full of *joy*.

90: For many years Abbas was a drug addict. He went to rehab twice, but every time he came back to drugs. He said Jesus was his last hope. The counselors prayed for him, and he accepted Jesus as His Lord. A month later, his wife called to give us the good news! Abbas was *changed*. Not only was he not using drugs anymore or abusing her, but he was very kind and loving to his family. His wife was very thankful, and she prayed to become a Christian, too.

91: Safar called Mohabat TV. He told the counselors that he asked Jesus two days ago to set him free from drugs. He said from that day forward, he didn't like drugs anymore. Safar gave his *heart* to Jesus with the counselors' help.

92: Bahram from Sari, Iran, was impacted by the programs on Mohabat TV. On the same day he accepted Jesus, he stopped smoking, drinking and cursing. Bahram said he had been smoking for twenty years! This was the *first* time that he was free.

93: Kobra was watching Mohabat TV talk about sigheh (temporary marriage in Iran). She was confused and called the counselors to argue. When they explained Jesus, His unfailing love and life-giving power, Kobra *accepted* Jesus. She said she would leave her temporary husband even though she has two children and her ex-husband is a drug addict.

94: Siamak left a message for the counselors to ask for prayer with his drug addiction. They called many times but no answer. His mom never picked up the phone because she was praying the Namaz. Finally, they got through and shared that salvation was only through Jesus Christ. After a long conversation with much reasoning, Siamak's mom gave her heart to the Lord. When Siamak came home from school, he *immediately* prayed to accept Jesus. He said, "We never watch Mohabat! We didn't even know there was a Christian channel." They were so touched by receiving Jesus, that they threw away everything pertaining to Islam including her Namaz prayers and the Quran. They said they would pray and talk only to Jesus from now on. Siamak's mom said that she had a Christian friend who always witnessed to her, but she never listened. She couldn't wait to call her friend and tell her that Jesus was in her heart now!

95: Mardin called Mohabat TV from Kurdistan. As a soldier, he had become addicted to alcohol. One day he watched a program, and, after accepting Jesus, Mardin called to testify that he is *free* from alcohol. God completely changed him.

96: Milad had a brother who was in prison for thirteen years because of his drug addiction. He called Mohabat TV asking for prayer and believed that Jesus could do this miracle. The next week Milad's brother was *released* from jail and so happy!

97: Nasrin called Mohabat TV to ask for prayer for her son who was a drug addict. She spoke to the counselors during a live show, and they prayed for her son. She couldn't stop sobbing. Nasrin called the next week with exciting news. Her son was *free* from drugs. She said he came home two days after she received prayer and said, "I don't want to turn to drugs anymore." He has been free ever since. Nasrin said she can see the change in him.

98: A young man named Arsalan was deep into drugs. He was using needles and was so addicted that the doctors said he had only six months to live. He was depressed but didn't have any strength to get off the drugs. He called Mohabat TV for help. He prayed with the counselors and accepted Jesus into his heart. The next few days, he felt better. He had no *desire* for drugs. He was wondering what happened, so he saw the doctor again. The doctor said that he was perfectly fine. Nothing was wrong with him. Arsalan was completely healed. He called the counselors back to say he is thankful to Jesus who gave him his life back. He said God blessed him financially. He now earns ten times his previous income. He is so full of joy even though his wife has left him to live with her mom. She calls Arsalan an "infidel" because he became a Christian and therefore is unclean.

99: Nahid was a drug addict to three different substances. She said she was ninety percent dead and ten percent alive due to the drugs. She became a Christian four years earlier and gave her heart to Jesus. The Lord began to restore her daily. When she thought she was dying, she asked God to "give me a tongue so I can tell them how you changed me if you save me." She says she tells everyone that it's been four years. She was once dead, but now Jesus made her alive. She called Mohabat TV because there was an atheist man in her neighborhood who was sick. She wasn't sure how to share the Gospel with him. The counselors prayed for her and encouraged her to share her testimony with him. That night, she called back. Because he felt Jesus's *compassion* and Nahid's care, he prayed to accept Jesus in his heart!

100: Ghazanfar was addicted to heroin. He tried everything to be free, but nothing helped his addiction. One night he was watching Mohabat TV and prayed to Jesus to help him be set free from his addiction. *Right* then, Ghazanfar passed out completely. When he woke up, he had no desire for any drugs. He called during a live show to proclaim his newfound freedom and then immediately prayed for salvation.

101: Reza's five year old son was watching Mohabat TV. He told his dad, "Dad, come. God is on TV!" A couple days earlier, Reza had prayed with the counselors and gave his life to Jesus. He called to asked for guidance on how to get free of his addiction. They prayed, and from then on he was free. Reza's whole family noticed the difference. When his son had severe back pain, he knew he could get healed by watching the TV. Reza gave his testimony during a live show of how God changed *everything* around.

102: Behnam, a young addict from Shiraz, Iran, called Mohabat TV crying. He couldn't talk, so his friend spoke for him. His friend explained that he felt miserable and wanted to be free from drug addiction. The counselors prayed, and

Behnam called back two days later saying that God changed him. His friends and family were so thankful that Behnam was so happy.

103: Sahar called Mohabat TV from Karaj, Iran, to ask for prayer for her nineteen-year-old son who was addicted to drugs. He was involved with a group of friends who were all addicts. They prayed with her, and she called a few months later to say her son had been healed. She gave her testimony during a live show that her son was free of drugs and had accepted Jesus in his heart. She said *everyone* who knows him was surprised by the mighty miracle Jesus performed in his life.

104: Isa was a Muslim who was addicted to drugs. He tried everything to get free off drugs, including going to shrines and giving donations to Imams to receive prayer. Nothing helped until he watched Mohabat TV. Isa called the counselors to ask for prayer. He gave his life to Jesus and is *forever* changed and free.

105: Mostafa called from Tehran, Iran, to give his testimony on a Mohabat TV live show. He was addicted to drugs for thirty-three years. Since he was seventeen, he spent fourteen years of his life in jail because of drugs. He and his fanatic Muslim family argued with his sister when she became a Christian three years ago. He tried arguing with her, too, but gave his life to Jesus *instead*. Now at fifty, he said he still struggles with drugs. He wasn't strong in his faith. He called to share with the counselors that he called on the name of Jesus in the middle of the night when he woke up in severe pain. He prayed, "Burn Satan in my life, in the name of Jesus." Three days after praying that prayer, Mostafa was completely free of drugs after being addicted for *thirty-three* years.

106: Roya and her husband were addicted to drugs for twenty-seven years. She watched *The Jesus Film* and gave her heart to Jesus. She was freed from drug addiction. She testified to her husband, and he believed in Jesus, too! He was also *freed*. She called Mohabat TV to testify how powerful our Lord is!

107: Reza from Mashhad, Iran, was moved by the testimonies on Mohabat TV. He called to give his life to Jesus. He was a drug addict and asked the counselors to pray for his freedom. A month later, Reza called crying. Since the night the counselors prayed for him, he hasn't *touched* drugs. Jesus completely changed him!

108: Mohsen called Mohabat TV from Esfahan, Iran, asking for prayer. His wife left him, and he was depressed. He tried to commit suicide several times by injecting heroine, but the Lord saved his life. Only thirty years old, Mohsen was addicted to drugs for seventeen years and spent five of those years in prison. He called back to say that Jesus delivered him from drugs since they prayed three weeks earlier. Mohsen was so happy and thankful for the prayers. He even told the doctors "the Living God" *healed* him.

109: Hadi became a believer through Mohabat TV. For the past six months, he had witnessed to his family. *All* six sons became believers, too! Hadi said he had many testimonies and miracles to report, but the best one, he says, was that two of his sons were completely free of drugs.

110: Sharareh called Mohabat TV for prayer. Her husband was in prison for drugs. The counselors prayed and invited her to accept Jesus. They also prayed for her husband. Sharareh called in few hours later, saying she just received news that her husband would be released from jail soon. She was so happy that Jesus answered her prayer so *quickly*.

111: Marzieh told the Mohabat TV counselors that after they prayed for her son, he was completely free from drugs. That made her so *happy* that she prayed to receive Christ as her Savior.

112: Robabeh's niece witnessed to her, and she accepted Jesus in her heart. She was sixty years old and called Mohabat TV with one request. She wanted the counselors to pray for her husband who was addicted to opium for twenty years. She called back fifteen days later to say that God answered her request. Her husband was freed *miraculously*. Robabeh said, "I know only Jesus could have healed him!"

113: Azadeh from Shiraz, Iran, was a drug addict. She watched Mohabat TV for two years until the programs helped her to be free from her addiction. Azadeh called the counselors to *receive* Christ as her Lord and Savior.

114: Fereshteh called Mohabat TV because she was an alcoholic and needed help. The counselors prayed for her while she cried. Fereshteh explained her rough life and why she needed God to intervene. She called a couple days later to say that she couldn't drink. Fereshteh said the desire was gone, and she was completely free. She said she felt complete *peace* and didn't want to fight with her family anymore.

115: Mohsen was a drug addict for thirty-five years. One night, he stumbled across Mohabat TV. He heard a testimony from a caller who praised Jesus for healing her son of cancer. Mohsen asked Jesus to heal him from his drug addiction. He said he would call in if he were healed like the lady's son. The next day, Mohsen went to use drugs—and all of a *sudden* he felt the need lift from him. Mohsen didn't desire drugs anymore. He called the counselors to testify on a live show about his miracle!

116: Hassan was an extreme drug addict. Nothing would satisfy him anymore. He used the strongest drugs available in the highest dosage, without any affect. He got to a point that he wanted to kill himself, but he failed in the attempt. Hassan's mother tried every prayer, religion, shrine and mosque, but nothing worked. One morning, Hassan found Mohabat TV while flipping through the channels. He heard Jesus could do miracles. He cried and prayed, "Jesus, if you can do miracles, you can free me of drugs." His tears fell on the drugs that laid on his lap, making a mess. He cleaned up the mess, wiped his tears away and took a shower. After he got dressed, he felt fresh, happy and could breathe easily. *Confused*, Hassan called the counselors to pray to receive Christ as His Lord and Savior.

117: Samee called Mohabat TV to tell the counselors that he had been *freed* from his drug addiction. He said, "I am blessed by each of your programs. It has been four years that I have trusted Jesus Christ. Jesus Christ changed my life. He saved my life from opium, hashish and nicotine. Let my testimony be heard by all people who are into drugs. You all need Jesus. He can save you and he can fill you instead with God's Spirit."

118: Sajjad, an Afghan living in Iran, called Mohabat TV. He said he grew up in a time of chaos. He tried his best to observe religion, but the more he tried, the more he was confused. Sajjad became addicted to drugs. He tried quitting but was so miserable when he tried to fill the void in his life. Hopeless, he started using drugs again. During this time, he found Mohabat TV. After watching the channel for two months, he accepted Jesus. As a result, a huge burden departed from his life. He became peaceful. After seeing the change, his entire family became believers. His brother Ali shared during a live show that: "I also wanted to thank my God that I have stepped into a new way in life. There are not enough words to thank God that I came to know the Living

God. I never had this kind of peace before. Yes, praise God, our entire family are believers now. Our hearts are now filled with love and joy. We love each other now. The touch of God's joy in us is truly amazing. We now talk with each other, regretting the time we wasted, wondering why we did not become believers of Jesus the Living God sooner. My mother and my two other brothers have also become Christians as a result. My older brother Sajjad testified about how his life was in a mess, but from the time he believed in Jesus, he was changed. He started to respect us and respect our parents. He is kind and loving now. We were all amazed at this change in him. At first, he hid his new faith from us, but after some time we came to him and asked him: 'What has happened to you Sajjad? Please let us in on the trick! What changed your life?' Finally, he spoke of his faith in Christ, and we all wanted to know more. I cannot really express myself properly about what is inside my heart. After we became believers, God performed another miracle in the life of our youngest brother who was sick for many years. He was healed, and, as a result, my mother became a believer. Our two other brothers living in Greece have also become Christians."

4: HUNGRY4LOVE

"Blessed are they that *hunger and thirst* after righteousness: for they shall be filled" (Matthew 5:6, emphasis added).

119: Amar from Kabul, Afghanistan, called Mohabat TV. He said, "Blessings to you. I am so glad that I can speak with you and watch your beautiful programs. It touches my heart every time I watch. It has been five years that I have been searching for a way to find peace to my *heart*. In this cause, I researched and also studied some books, and I have come to a point today that Christ is the only answer I have to a lasting peace and joy in my life. I am so glad that during my research one day, I found your program, and this the reason that I called today. I am so thankful to God, and I believe in my heart that the Gospel of Christ has touched my life. There are problems in my life and in Afghanistan. People call themselves the followers of a true religion, but Islam cannot answer my questions and voids. Today, I am asking for you to pray for me so that I can receive Jesus into my heart." The counselors prayed this prayer with Amar and his family, who also prayed to receive Christ. "Dear Lord, I thank you for your love for me. Dear God, I thank you for sending Jesus Christ for my salvation. Dear Lord, I confess to and repent my sins before you. I believe that Jesus Christ died for my sake. He died on the cross and was buried, but on the third day, He rose again from the dead. Dear Lord Jesus Christ, I am requesting you to please come into my heart. Become the Lord and Savior of my life, Amen."

120: Mojtaba called Mohabat TV and gave his heart to the Lord. His life has changed so much that he witnessed to his friends at the university. Almost *seventy* people accepted Jesus through Mojtaba. They were all excited and full of joy.

121: Hossein called Mohabat TV from Kermanshah, Iran. He graduated from Islamic theology and was working to become a Molah. He came across the channel and had been watching it for few weeks. Hossein called to ask more questions about Christianity. He asked to get the Bible so he could study for himself. Once he read the Bible, he called us to say he was sure Jesus was the true God. He *thanked* us from his heart for sending us the "precious" Word.

122: Amir was an orphan. He called Mohabat TV wanting to know more about Jesus' divinity. The counselors explained the trinity, and after many calls and questions, Amir finally gave his heart to the Lord. He had always hated God for putting him through his messy life. Now, Amir was *born again!* He loved how much God changed him that he proclaimed to all his friends about Jesus's love.

123: Dariush called Mohabat TV from Tehran, Iran. He asked for a Bible and wanted to know about Christianity. The counselors explained, and he asked to pray to accept Jesus. They prayed with him, and Dariush was full of joy. He started weeping because he knew the truth. He said he couldn't explain it, but he felt that God sent Mohabat TV to tell him the truth in his heart.

124: A woman watched Mohabat TV and was touched by one of the testimonies. She called in asking to speak to the woman who gave her testimony. The counselors asked if she was a Christian. She said no, but she wanted to know more. They explained to the woman that salvation was only through Jesus Christ. The woman *believed.* She prayed with the counselors to give her life to the Lord. She thanked us for the testimonies that changed her heart.

125: Kia was an angry man who often called Mohabat TV to harass and curse at the counselors. He continued calling with many questions. Finally, after getting the answers he wanted, he asked one of the counselors to pray with him to receive salvation. Kia gave his *heart* to the Lord. He no longer cursed or felt angry enough to harass anymore.

126: Hamid called Mohabat TV from Baloochestan, Iran. He said he had no hope. When he tried talking to God in Islam, he got no answer. He got divorced and remarried in the hope of finding a better life. No use! Hamid started to hate religion. He was very broke, living in a village outside town, but got himself a satellite dish. He came across Mohabat TV and started enjoying the programs. Hamid was curious about Christianity. One night he called the counselors, and his *whole* family accepted Jesus in their hearts!

127: Kamran was a very broken man. He called Mohabat TV to explain that he was addicted to drugs, committing adultery and had AIDS. Kamran asked if his relationships with women were wrong? The counselors explained sin and salvation through Jesus Christ. He believed in his heart and left the women he was seeing. He called the live show to testify on air that he believed God *healed* him of AIDS.

128: Behzad only had one hand. He thought if he called Mohabat TV and became a Christian, he could ask them for money. The counselors explained Jesus would provide for him if he asked with his whole heart. Behzad accepted Christ, and received prayer for his financial situation. He called back the next day, excited that he found a job. He praised God at how quickly He provided.

129: Elham gave her heart to Jesus during a Mohabat TV program. She said everything she prayed to God in her heart were answered. She shared with the counselors that God answered her prayers for her father's financial situation within a few days. He is now debt *free*.

130: A widowed woman with a fifth grade education felt lonely. There was no support or financial aid for her, and she was in desperate need. One evening she came to the end of her rope while watching Mohabat TV. She began to scream and cry loudly and asked God for help. She said even though it was night, a small beam of light shown in her living room. When Mohabat TV came on the television, suddenly the entire room filled with light and the shape of a cross appeared in front of her. The woman knew the cross was related to Christianity. She got on her knees and began to *worship* Jesus. The following day, a man showed up at the front of her house. He said God told him to give her a certain amount of money. She told him she couldn't accept it because she didn't know him. The man persuaded her that one day she would reimburse him. That money helped her to stand on her feet. She called the counselors to accept Jesus in her heart. The woman said she never saw that man again. She shared the Word of God with her daughter and son-in-law after her miracle and continues to share with anyone who comes in her path.

131: Shahram gave his life to Jesus a few months ago while watching Mohabat TV. He called to testify that he doesn't smoke anymore, commit adultery or have bad thoughts since he became a Christian. Shahram said Jesus not only forgave *all* his sins, but cleansed his heart from sinful deeds as well. He was so happy over how much his life changed!

132: Hamid was sick of life. He tried committing suicide a number of times, but it didn't work. The last time, he put a gun in his mouth but didn't have the heart to shoot. He found the Mohabat TV channel and called to ask for prayer. The counselor who picked up the phone was so filled with God's power and presence that she started crying and talking to Hamid about God's love without letting him explain his story or knowing anything about his background. She led Hamid to pray and accept Jesus as his Lord and Savior. Then he shared his story with her. Hamid said he had nobody in his life. His parents divorced and abandoned him. He didn't go to school because of his lack of money. He thought no one loved him, but today he said he *found* out that one person who does love him is Jesus!

133: Salar was a very angry man. He was always mad at life. He found Mohabat TV and heard that people received prayer for peace. Salar called the counselors and asked if his life could be peaceful. They prayed and explained that Jesus could give him peace beyond his understanding. Salar accepted Jesus but was doubtful if he would ever change. One day driving on the freeway his car broke down, and while he was waiting for help, Salar realized he wasn't *mad*! He didn't get angry at the situation and lifted his hand to Jesus in middle of the freeway, praising the Lord for peace. He was a changed man!

134: A man called Mohabat TV to say he watched the programs faithfully for two years. He called to the counselors to ask them a question. "Do you know why the cross is empty?" Without waiting for them to answer, he said, "Because He is in my heart now!" The counselors were amazed at his spiritual growth. Since he never "officially" prayed the prayer of salvation, one of the counselors prayed with him. Even though he was an illiterate seventy-five-year-old man, he learned *all* the life giving truths by watching Mohabat TV faithfully.

135: Lieli, an Afghan living in Iran, spoke to the counselors at Mohabat TV. She said, "I just called you to let you know that it has been fifteen days since I trusted in the Lord Jesus Christ. *Everything* that I have asked the Lord Jesus Christ, He has given me. My heart is so thankful to Him."

136: Aref was confused about the true "God." He went on his house roof and prayed, "Lord, everyone says different things about who You are. But I want to know the truth. You tell me who is right!" Aref came down and happened to turn on his TV to Mohabat. They were showing *The Jesus Film*. Aref was surprised that God answered him so quickly, and that Jesus is God. He prayed, "Jesus, if you are the True God, please send someone to tell me!" Aref's phone *rang*! A Mohabat TV counselor called to tell him about Jesus. He sobbed and cried while praying to accept Jesus in his heart as his Lord and Savior!

137: Zainab from Afghanistan emailed Mohabat TV saying, "I watched today's show. I heard the testimony of sister Zohra, and it touched my heart so much. I am a Muslim, but I have been watching your TV show for a long time. Today when I heard sister Zohra, I was encouraged to contact you. Would you please pray for me? I have suffered in my life as well. I still live and work in Afghanistan. Today when I heard sister Zohra, I really am now interested in the *Bible*."

138: Darab called Mohabat TV and said, "I have a problem and I want you to pray for me. I got divorced, but I want to go back to my wife. But the devil doesn't let us. I have been watching your show for a few months, and I *believe* in God. I strongly believe Him." The counselors prayed the salvation prayer with him over the phone, and he accepted Jesus in his heart.

139: After Maryam watched Mohabat TV for the first time, she called the counselors for help. She recently got divorced one year ago. Her husband had already remarried. She said, "I want you pray to Jesus for me to take me back to my kids. I am fasting, and I asked God too many times, but He didn't answer me. Now I want Christ to do something for me. I want to go back to my kids and my life. I am asking God, going to mosque and fasting. I am young and thirty years old, but I can't hear anything. I want to tell you our religious activities are not things to give us peace. None of the religious activities give us peace. I am tired of religion. I am looking for a relationship with God. Can you help me, please?" The counselors explained the *simplicity* of the Gospel. She said, "You mean in Christianity, if a little bit of my hair comes out of my head covering I am not in sin? Or if I shake hands with a man?" Maryam was in total amazement. She said, "I want to evangelize about 'Jesus religion'! How can I become a pastor?" With all her heart, she accepted Jesus as her Lord and Savior. Maryam, hungry for the Gospel, has already shared with her cousin and her classmate.

140: A woman called Mohabat TV in deep sadness and said, "I have three prayer requests. I want my goldfish to stay alive, my head never to get injured as my husband hits my head all the time, and that our landlord doesn't throw us away as my husband and I are fighting." The woman said her husband was always hitting her and using drugs. She said, "I need another year to find a place to live. I am an orphan and without any family. That's why I got married." The counselors asked why she asked them to pray for her goldfish. The woman said, "They are my pets. I speak to them and care about them and love them very much." She said her *fish* were the only source of soothing her loneliness until that day when she received Jesus as her Lord and Savior in her heart.

141: Mashalah called Mohabat TV to thank the counselors for praying for his land in the village. He said, "The blessings of the Lord came upon it. I had a great *harvest* compared to previous years and compared to other famers in my village." The counselors prayed with Mashalah, his friend, wife and family who all got saved after this miracle!

142: Fataneh found Mohabat TV one night and liked it at first. She watched until she heard things contrary to her beliefs. Fataneh's husband was a drug addict who would beat her, tie her to a chair and lock her up in a room by herself. This continued for years until she remembered Mohabat TV said Jesus could save her, and nothing was too hard for Him. During an abusive night when her husband was hitting her, she called on the name of Jesus. Her husband made fun of her and said, "Let's see if this Jesus can help you!" He tied her up, double locked the door and hid the keys. That night she prayed to *Jesus* with her whole heart. For the first time in her life, she asked the Lord for help. She said, "As they said on Mohabat TV, you promised to help and answer our prayers. So please release me from this prison!" As she was praying, she felt the ropes loosen on her hand. Suddenly she knew where the keys were. She found them and opened the door. She escaped to her mom's house. The next day, Fataneh's husband went looking for her, only to find she was free. Since that day, Fataneh always prays to Jesus. She called the counselors at Mohabat TV and asked how she could become Christian. Her husband is afraid to do anything against her because of the new power in her.

5: RESTORING RELATIONSHIPS

"Blessed are the *merciful*: for they shall obtain mercy"
(Matthew 5:7, emphasis added).

143: Fatemeh was engaged to be married when her fiancé called Mohabat TV to give his heart to Jesus with the counselors over the phone. He handed Fatemeh the phone so she could become a Christian, too. Fatemeh didn't want to pray, and she asked the counselors many questions. When they explained the Gospel to her, and that Jesus is the only one who can forgive sins, she cried. Fatemeh said, "I have been asking my prophet Mohammad, Imam Ali, and others in Islam to forgive my sins and help me, but nobody did. I asked God to show me the truth and you called. You are an *answer* to my prayers!" Fatemeh joyfully accepted Jesus.

144: A couple called Mohabat TV from Tehran, Iran. They both got saved and requested prayer. The wife said, "I lost my sister nineteen years ago. Right now, I know this living God, Jesus, hears our prayers. Can you please pray for me so that I can find my sister?" The counselors prayed for her, and a few hours later the husband cried for joy. "This is a miracle, this is a miracle. The Lord Jesus did this miracle. It is amazing, so amazing. My wife found her sister after nineteen years. Please let your church know. Please let *all* people know that Jesus did it." The counselor shared this with two of her church members who called to say that the husband's brother was lost on the streets of Tehran. He had a disease and often forgot where he was. For the past two days, his family was in tears. The counselor shared the story about the couple finding the wife's sister, and she prayed for them. *Exactly* twenty minutes after they prayed, he called back with joy and tears that someone found his brother on the streets of Tehran. He witnessed to his family in Iran as they are not saved yet.

145: A man watching Mohabat TV last year felt the anointing of the Lord come upon him while watching the programs. He called the counselors to say he had been delivered from homosexuality *completely*. The man said his journey of relationships began with Jesus!

146: Ehtesham called Mohabat TV, and asked the counselors to pray for his problems with his wife. They prayed for his salvation, along with his relationship with his wife. Two weeks later, Ehtesham called and said, "I somehow feel changed! My relationship with my wife is much *better*." Ehtesham was happy to become a Christian.

147: Nasrin watched Mohabat TV for a couple of months before she finally called to ask the counselors to pray for her to get pregnant. She said, "I believe Jesus is the only one who can answer my prayer!" Nasrin prayed with her husband to receive Christ as her Lord and Savior. She called two months later, rejoicing that Jesus answered her prayer. Nasrin was *pregnant!* She told her family and doctor that Jesus answered her prayers and gave her a baby.

148: Mohammad often called the counselors at Mohabat TV to harass and flirt with them. The counselors explained Jesus was the only way to God and listened to his many questions. Mohammad was touched. He confessed he was in a relationship with a married woman. He also said he was into drugs, and his main purpose for calling was to bother the counselors. They explained that Satan wants to steal, kill and destroy—but Jesus would give him *abundant* life if he repented. Mohammad repented and accepted Jesus as his Lord.

149: Shahin called Mohabat TV from Esfahan, Iran. She said her husband was committing adultery, and she was very angry. She asked the counselors to pray for her and her husband. They prayed and followed up with her many times. After three weeks of prayer, Shahin called back to say that her husband was back *home*!

150: Aseyah, an Afghan lady from Holland, called Mohabat TV to give her heart to Jesus. She called to ask for prayer multiple times for her husband who would leave her for other women. Aseyah called back so excited to let the counselors know that her husband was back! He had even *apologized* to her and was willing to go to church.

151: Mehdi and Maryam were separating. Mehdi called Mohabat TV for prayer. He was going to kill himself because she was already with another man. The counselors talked with Maryam, and she gave her heart to Jesus. Mehdi and Maryam got back together! Mehdi said, "It is only God's grace" that he *forgave* her and did not commit suicide.

152: Shahrokh was a very angry man when he called Mohabat TV. He asked if "our Jesus" could do anything about his anger because it had ruined his family. The counselors explained the Good News and told him to give all his burdens to Jesus because He cared for him. Shahrokh prayed and asked Jesus in His heart. He called the next day, saying he felt peaceful. He couldn't wait to bring his wife and children back home to live *peacefully* with them.

153: Reza called Mohabat TV to speak with one of the host pastors. He said he was sexually abused by his father from very early childhood. Reza was touched by the programs and called to receive Christ. He called back to say how Jesus has changed his life and claimed he felt so *free* from sin! Reza said he couldn't even lie. He said, "I don't know what is wrong with me!"

154: A Muslim lady called Mohabat TV. She had many questions about Jesus and Him being God. She called many times and kept questioning the counselors. Finally, the lady's husband spoke to the counselors and accepted Jesus. Eventually, the lady and their children accepted the Lord. Wherever her husband goes, he calls the counselors and asks them to pray for his friends and relatives to receive Christ. So far, because of this lady's husband, at least *thirty* people have come to faith in Christ.

155: Akram called Mohabat TV from Tehran, Iran. She was always mad and angry. She was on the verge of a divorce. Akram's husband wanted to leave her because of her rage and violence. She prayed to receive Christ with the counselors, and when her husband saw the *change* in her, they both dedicated their life to Jesus. They fasted and prayed for their son who was tormented by nightmares, and he was healed!

156: One day husband and wife, Mahmood and Malihe, watched Mohabat TV with four fortune tellers. They called the counselors to talk about relationships and ask for guidance. Mahmood said he liked another woman. He believed it was okay to love other women besides his wife. The counselors explained the Gospel to Mahmood and Malihe, who prayed to receive Christ. They handed the phone to the four fortune tellers, and they *all* prayed to receive Christ as well. The fortune tellers said they were leaving their line of work, and promised to follow Jesus the true God!

157: Ali called Mohabat TV to ask the counselors to pray for his family. He had questions about Christianity. The counselors answered, and Ali gave his heart to the Lord. He called back to say he was a very bitter man in the past, and that is why his wife left him and took the children. Ali said God changed him, and he is very kind now. His wife is so happy that God changed Ali, his life, his family—and *everything*.

158: Mojtaba called Mohabat TV and gave his heart to the Lord with the counselors. He said that God changed him and his wife and blessed their family. Mojtaba had a court situation, and had asked the counselors for prayer. He said the judge favored him in court, and he was forgiven. He got the answer to his prayers. Mojtaba couldn't stop rejoicing and thanking Jesus for this major *victory* in his life.

159: Eysa called Mohabat TV from Karaj, Iran, to gave his life to Jesus. He had prayed all of his life to find his real family. One year later, the counselors called back to follow up with Eysa. He was so happy to announce that he found his family after *fifteen* years of searching! Jesus answered his prayer.

160: Mahboubeh, a seventy-two year old woman, accepted Jesus Christ as her Lord and Savior with the counselors at Mohabat TV. In the beginning of the Islamic revolution, Mahboubeh's son-in-law and pregnant daughter were assassinated by the government. For years, she said she could not forgive the killers. Mahboubeh was full of hate. When she accepted Jesus, the Lord *healed* her. It took some time, but Mahboubeh was able to forgive, and, as a result, she is now filled with peace.

161: Hamid called Mohabat TV asking for prayer for his wife. They were separated and tried everything to solve their financial problems. Hamid was a religious and devout man who ministered in the mosque. One night he was so fed up with life, he flipped through TV channels and came across Mohabat. Hamid watched and listened very carefully. He asked Jesus to come to his heart and to fix his messed up life. He told Jesus he wanted to live with his wife again. He later shared with the counselors how grateful he was that Jesus answered his requests. He was now living with his wife again, and their financial problems were *solved.* Hamid says he is now thankful because whatever he has is from the Lord!

162: Maryam was a single mother of two children and very angry and fed up with life. After her husband left her, she was more frustrated, so she went to many psychologists. But none helped! Maryam started watching Mohabat TV and called for prayer and gave her life to Jesus. Ever since then, she said her life changed. She has joy in her life and loves her children. She even apologized to her husband, too.

163: Ebrahim was in prison when his wife witnessed to him. She told him that she watched Mohabat TV and became a Christian. Ebrahim listened and thought about Jesus. The next day, he was miraculously released. He called our counselors and gave his life to the Lord *immediately*. He not only stopped doing drugs, he even stopped smoking cigarettes. Ebrahim says Jesus healed, *restored* and blessed his family with so much joy.

164: Mahtab's husband, Fazel, called Mohabat TV. He wanted to become a Christian. The counselors explained the Gospel, and prayed with him to receive Christ. After two days, Mahtab called and wanted to know what the counselors told her husband. She said he was changed! He no longer gets violent or angry at home. She said the whole family felt joy and unusual peace that was now upon Fazel. Mahtab prayed to receive Christ with all *three* of their children. She thanked Mohabat TV so much because their lives have changed for the better.

165: Fariba called Mohabat TV from Sweden to talk with the Afghan host during a live show. She said, "I am a Muslim convert to Christ from Iran. When I was a Muslim and lived in Iran, I witnessed the brutal killing of a family by an Afghan man. From that time onward, I hated even the name Afghan or Afghanistan. Years later when I turned to Jesus Christ, many changes came to my life. But, I still continued be uncomfortable with Afghans. One day while trying to change channels on my remote, I came across Mohabat TV.

Immediately I knew from your accent that you aı
so I switched the TV off. A few hours later, I ‹
and switched on the TV again. Lo and behold
your show being repeated on Mohabat TV. I sʹ
again. Another day, I came across your show and watched
some. Wanting to switch it off again, God knocked on my
heart. He said, 'Fariba, what are you doing?' With a lot of
courage, I started to watch your show even though half-
hearted. As weeks passed by and I heard God's Word from
you, God spoke to me, and now I always look forward to
your show. It has become my *favorite* TV show. God has
healed me and has used your show in my life. Now I love my
Afghan brothers and sisters. I pray for you and I pray for the
Afghans and pray for Afghanistan. Today I called you to ask
your forgiveness and to please pray for me. I am asking God
to forgive me for having had such an attitude toward my
Afghan brothers and sister, and through this show today I am
requesting the Afghans to please forgive me."

166: A woman called Mohabat TV to share how blessed she
was from watching the programs. She said her sister, Nahid,
and her children called the counselors to give their hearts to
Jesus Christ as well. Their mom and other sister became a
believer, too. She said her whole family became Christians
because of the change in her heart and life. She said Jesus
Christ transformed her and did a miracle in her life. The
woman said she used to curse and insult everyone. Now her
tongue has become the *praying* tongue, and she loves
everyone.

167: A young man was so touched by the power of the Holy
Spirit during the prayer of salvation with the counselors at
Mohabat TV that he just wept while they prayed with him.
He said that he had "a silver tongue," but now he was like a
mute. The man was so overwhelmed by Jesus's love, peace
and joy. He couldn't believe that his wife had just gotten
saved *one* day before when she, too, called Mohabat TV!

.68: A man watched Mohabat TV about witchcraft. He called to testify how fortune-telling ruined his life. He said his wife had consulted a fortune teller years ago. The fortune teller told his wife that one day he would marry a second wife. She believed the lie for thirteen years. Later on, the man's wife committed adultery and left him for a married man. During this time, the man blamed himself for believing Satan's lies and letting them torture his mind. He confessed that he blamed God for everything that happened to him and his son. Although the man forgave his wife, he sometimes felt the urge to take vengeance. He said after watching Mohabat TV, the Lord set him free. After the man prayed a salvation prayer, he said, "I feel so *light*. I feel in my heart a sense of true forgiveness."

6: DARE TO DREAM

"Blessed are the *pure in heart*: for they shall see God"
(Matthew 5:8, emphasis added).

169: Roghiyeh called Mohabat TV to pray to receive Christ with the counselors after what happened to her. The night her brother gave her a necklace of Jesus on the cross, she had a dream. Roghiyeh dreamed Jesus was looking at her while He was on the cross. The next day, Roghiyeh said she went to see the Mullah (Islamic clergy man) to ask him about the dream. In total amazement, he replied, "That was Imam Ali on the cross you saw, not the prophet Jesus." Roghiyeh said that she replied, "I am sure Imam Ali was not crucified and didn't die like that. Only Jesus died on the cross." Roghiyeh said even the Mullah laughed at his own answer! She was *absolutely* sure that Jesus died for her sins. Roghiyeh couldn't wait to give her heart to Jesus.

170: Narges had a dream a few months after watching Mohabat TV. She called the counselors to ask what it meant. She said that Jesus gave her a cup of His blood, and the Holy Spirit told her to use it for salvation. They explained the blood of Jesus, and how it was shed for her sins. Narges gave her life to Jesus and said the fear of Islam left *immediately*!

171: Nahid called Mohabat TV to ask for prayer for her niece who disappeared seven months prior. The counselors shared about a similar case, and after sharing the testimony of the other families, Nahid's faith increased. They prayed and believed God that Nahid would hear from her niece. A few days later, Nahid had a visitation from the Lord. He spoke to her. Twenty days later, Nahid's niece *called*. She was well and apologized for disappearing.

172: Maryam called Mohabat TV for prayer because her husband was a severe drug addict. The counselors prayed and explained the Gospel. Maryam accepted and prayed for salvation. That night she was praying by herself when all of a sudden she saw Jesus! She passed out. Jesus told her, "Follow me, and I will take care of everything!" When Maryam gained consciousness, she had an overwhelming peace. She said all her anxiousness was gone and she was in complete *rest*!

173: Hassan was addicted to drugs for twelve years. He sold all his family's furniture and appliances to satisfy his addiction. As a result, his wife left him. He was in a very bad financial situation, including many other problems he had because of his addiction. One night Hassan dreamt of an old man with white hair telling him to believe in Jesus. After watching Mohabat TV, he called the counselors and gave his heart to Jesus. Hassan said his life *changed*. He was delivered from his drug addiction and healed of all his diseases.

174: Mansour called Mohabat TV to say he prayed during one of the shows to ask Jesus to free him from drug addiction. For the next two nights, Mansour saw visions of Jesus and His love in his dreams. Mansour couldn't stop crying because God *freed* him from his drug addiction.

175: Ahmad was at the peak of his drug addiction three years ago. He said he asked Allah and the Islamic Imams for help. Instead, Ahmad said he got worse. He wanted to commit suicide. A friend advised him to ask God. Ahmad prayed, and Jesus came to him in a dream and said, "I have been watching over you, and protecting you all this time. I want you healed and *whole*. Follow me." Ahmad called Mohabat TV to give his testimony during a live show.

176: Ali called Mohabat TV and introduced himself as a Shiite Muslim. He said he needed prayers. Ali had been a drug dealer for a long time and grew up in a very devoted Islamic family with five brothers. He said he was the "black sheep" of the family. Ali was buying opium from Zahedan, Iran, to sell it for lots of money. No matter how much he made, he said he lost it all. Once in the middle of Kerman road, he got caught carrying 122 kilograms (about 269 pounds) of drugs. Ali was arrested and spent seven years in prison. No one cared or came to visit him except his wife. After Ali was released from prison, he watched Mohabat TV. When he heard about Jesus, he wept. Ali told Jesus that if He rescued and freed him from his lifestyle of misery, he would accept the "Jesus religion" in his heart and follow Him. Jesus heard Ali's request and delivered him from drug addiction. Ali had a dream a few months later. He said in his dream someone was standing with a cross and told him, "Did you forget the promise you made me?" The following morning, Ali saw his sons wearing cross necklaces! He was so surprised that he took it as a sign. While he watched Mohabat TV, he called to ask for prayer. Ali thought he needed to find a church building where he could say the prayer of repentance and salvation. After the counselors explained to the Gospel to him, he prayed over the phone and got saved. His sons were *excited* because they, too, had become followers of Jesus.

177: Ahmad called Mohabat TV from Hamedan, Iran. He said he gave his heart to Jesus three years ago but struggled with drugs. One night Jesus came to his dream and spoke with him. When he woke up, he said he was a *new* person full of light and joy. Ahmad said he no longer desires drugs.

178: Samad was addicted to drugs for many years. He was flipping channels in Gazvin, Iran, when he came across Mohabat TV. He stopped when he saw the host talking about drug addictions. Samad called in to explain he had been addicted to drugs for a long time and couldn't get free. He was fed up, disgusted and desperate for help. Samad wondered if Jesus could help him. The counselors explained that Jesus is God and that only He could do the impossible. Samad prayed and opened his heart for Jesus. Three days later, he said Jesus appeared to him in a dream. Jesus asked him to give his heart and life completely to Jesus, and that He would take care of the rest. When he woke up the next day, Samad felt completely *free*. He no longer desired drugs. Samad called to testified that Jesus can do the impossible indeed!

179: Milad joined the army and became addicted to all kinds of drugs. When he left the army, he was addicted to heroin. He was able to go to rehab, and one night Milad saw a vision. In the midst of darkness, he saw the sun. This great light came down and embraced him. The next morning, Milad was free of drugs. He told everyone that Jesus set him free, but nobody believed him. He said he felt very strong and had a *peace* he never experienced before.

180: Saeid called Mohabat TV to say that his friend saw Jesus in person. He became a Christian as a result and told all of his friends including Saeid. Saeid told the counselors that he, too, prayed to see Jesus face to face. He said that he saw Jesus' face in a rainbow, and that all the other friends of his friend have seen Jesus in different ways as well. He said that some of his friends were afraid to call the counselors, but many of them have come to faith in Jesus as a result of seeing Him!

181: Ester fell off a ledge and couldn't walk. She prayed that Jesus would heal her. After months of suffering and not walking, Jesus came to her in a dream and said, "Wait for May 13th, and I will heal you." The counselors shared with her about Jesus' resurrection, and Ester believed Jesus could heal her. She called back and gave her "resurrection day" testimony on the air!

182: Faranak called Mohabat TV from Chaloos, Iran. She had a tumor behind her head and couldn't move her arm. One night in a dream, she saw a cross and a bright man standing next to it. He was very bright so that she could only see his face and the outline of his figure. Faranak recognized Jesus by the cross next to him. He said, "Give me your hand." She stretched the paralyzed arm that she couldn't move. And as she stretched, Faranak was completely healed. The next morning she explained the dream to her family. Her family realized she was moving her paralyzed arm and pointed it out to her. That's when Faranak realized she was healed. Six years later, she found Mohabat TV. Faranak called the counselors to pray to receive Christ for the first time, and they sent her a Bible.

183: Mojahed called Mohabat TV to say he saw Jesus come out of the sea. The seashore was very dirty, but when Jesus stepped on the shore, everything was clean and full of grass. Mojahed walked toward Him, but Jesus stopped him and said, "You are not holy because you haven't confessed your sins." Jesus showed His hands to Mojahed. He asked Jesus for forgiveness and felt so light and happy that his sins were *forgiven.*

184: Rahman called Mohabat TV to pray for salvation. He said while his wife was sleeping, someone shook her to wake up and told her to believe in Jesus. Rahman's wife got up and watched Mohabat TV. She immediately came to faith. He said she was changed ever since. Rahman said he *loved* seeing the joy in his wife, and called to accept Jesus too. He was so happy.

185: Khadijeh did not want to believe in Christ. She knew of Mohabat TV and vowed to never believe in Christ or even talk to a Christian. One day at work, Khadijeh said she encountered Jesus at work from behind her desk. For half an hour, she saw Jesus Himself. All He said was "Don't doubt;

just believe." Khadijeh was confused. She called the counselors to ask why Jesus would show Himself to her. They explained, and Khadijeh confessed that she knew the Gospel but always refused to believe. This time, Jesus Himself asked her to *believe*! She cried while she repeated the salvation prayer. At first it was hard for her to repeat the salvation prayer, but as she was sobbing the words became easier for her. Khadijeh said, "I am free now, because I don't have to fight against God anymore!"

186: Shirin had two dreams within a couple of months. In both dreams, she was in a horrifying situation. In the first dream, Shirin was in prison witnessing her family's death. In the second dream, she was beheaded. In both dreams, Jesus came to her rescue and saved her and her family. Shirin called Mohabat TV to ask the counselors to interpret her dreams. They explained, and said that Jesus is the only one who can save us from death and eternal damnation. Shirin prayed to receive Christ, and after the prayer she was *released* of the fear and torment from her dreams.

187: Mohammad prayed his Muslim Namaz when his little daughter turned on the TV and listened to Mohabat. She told him, "Dad, this is the true prayer, not your Namaz!!" Mohammad still continued his Namaz but actually listened to the host. While still praying, Mohammad prayed to Jesus to solve a problem he was battling. After a week, he called the counselors to say that Jesus *answered* his prayer! He had a dream that he was lost in a desert and Jesus found him. They explained the Gospel, and Mohammad prayed to receive Jesus for his salvation.

188: One night, Mina heard a manly voice urging her to wake up from her deep sleep. After ignoring the voice a couple times, she was literally shaken to get out of bed! When she got up, she smelled gas all around the house. Mina woke up the rest of her family. She shut off the main gas line to the house and called the authorities. A while later, Mina heard about Jesus and gave her heart to Him. She realized that it was *He* who woke her up and saved her and her family. Mina changed so much in her walk with Jesus that everyone noticed and accepted Jesus, too!

189: Mahnaz called Mohabat TV to ask about tithing. She had a dream the night before that a man in a white gown appeared and opened a big pot. He took a bowl for himself and said the rest is yours. While Mahnaz watched Mohabat, the discussion was about tithing, and she always wondered why her husband had a good job and income, but they were not blessed. Mahnaz told the counselors, "From now on, I am *happy* to put aside a tenth of our income for the Lord."

190: An Afghan man saw Jesus in a vision, and he called Mohabat TV to say, "My whole life is *transformed*, and I want to live for Jesus."

191: Roya called Mohabat TV from Shiraz, Iran, to talk to a counselor. She had cancer, and her sister who was a believer prayed for her healing and witnessed to her. Roya didn't believe, but she asked God to show her a miracle. One evening while she was awake, she saw a vision. God told her he wanted to operate on her heart. She argued that she had cancer and needed healing. The Lord said that he needed to change her heart first and give her new life. Then He would heal her. Roya said Jesus healed her. She is completely healed and, most importantly, *born again*.

192: A woman saw a light in her dream, and this light told her to read John 15. She didn't know what John was. The woman watched Mohabat TV and heard them reading from the book of John. She called the counselors to get a Bible so she could start *reading* and accepted Jesus.

193: Hussain, an old Afghan man, called Mohabat TV to argue that no Afghan could become a Christian. The counselors explained salvation is through Jesus only, but he kept arguing. They challenged him to ask God to show him the truth. Hussain prayed and asked Jesus to reveal Himself. He did! Jesus came to his room in a bright light holding a cross, and told him, "I am the only one who can forgive sins." Hussain called back the *next* day to pray to receive Christ in his heart.

194: Ali from Shiraz, Iran, was always sick with a weak body. He never had peace of mind and couldn't find work or easy jobs. Ali felt stuck at home and was mad at everyone. He would break dishes and couldn't talk to anyone without breaking into a fight. One night, Jesus came to him in a dream and took him by the hand to lift him from the bed. Jesus introduced Himself and said He came to heal him. Ali said the next morning, he woke up and felt great. He was completely healed. Ali didn't know anything about Jesus and started watching Mohabat. He called the counselors to accept Jesus. He said he can *now* work, actually has friends and is at peace with everyone.

195: Farzad, a sixteen-year-old high school student, wasn't interested in Christianity at all because he was a devout Muslim. One day, his brother's friend said he had become a Christian. Farzad was touched. He prayed, "God if you are Jesus, prove it to me." He had a dream *that* night that Jesus was healing everyone who asked Him. When Farzad woke up, he prayed and asked Jesus, "If this is true, heal my eyes so I don't have to wear these glasses anymore." Jesus healed his eyes, and he is a witness to everyone. Farzad said he was very angry all the time and always looking for trouble. But now he has the peace of God on him. Everyone noticed his change, and his teacher testified that Farzad is a completely different man.

196: Basir called Mohabat TV because he wanted to argue during a live show because he was not convinced. He called again to argue with the counselors and challenged them to convince him once again so he could believe Jesus was God. Without any success, Basir hung up. He called back ten days later to say Jesus, Himself, appeared to him in a dream and answered *all* his questions. He cried and said, "He changed my life, and I am ready to do anything for our Lord Jesus Christ!"

197: Ali called Mohabat TV with a lot of problems. He was in so much stress that he tried to commit suicide. Ali threw himself in front of a speeding car to kill himself, when he saw Jesus standing in front of him. Ali said Jesus stopped him, told him to get up and said, "Go, and my peace will be with you." Ali told the counselors that Jesus had *saved* him from death. He then asked what he should do to become a Christian.

198: Arash called Mohabat TV from Gilan, Iran. He asked the counselors to interpret his dreams. He had many visions about Jesus, Jesus being raptured and Jesus talking to him. The counselors explained the Gospel, and Arash *accepted* the Lord.

199: Alireza called Mohabat TV to share his testimony. One day while having dinner, Jesus entered and ate with them. He introduced Himself as God and Savior. When Alireza found Mohabat TV, he called and said, "I know your God." He was so excited that Jesus loved him so much that He cared to spend time with him and his family.

200: Soheila always watched Mohabat TV, but she was very confused as to which religion was the right way to God: Islam or Christianity? One night she had a dream where she heard someone tell her she was going the wrong way. From then on, Sohelia watched Mohabat TV more often. She had severe back pain, and, during a show where they were praying for the sick, she was healed. Sohelia's son called to pray with the counselors, and he was healed! He no longer needed an operation. Sohelia called during a live show to give her testimony and heart to the Lord.

201: Morteza worked in the Imam Reza temple. He had a dream where Jesus called him to the light. He called Mohabat TV to ask the counselors what that meant and what he should do. The counselors directed him to pray for salvation. Days later, Morteza called to say that his family wanted to pray for *salvation*, too! They had noticed his change.

202: Aref from Shoosh, Iran, was very happy to call Mohabat TV and ask for a Bible. He had a dream that he and his wife had two baskets of dry fish, and living water was coming from the television set for them to drink. Aref woke up and wondered what his dream meant. He prayed that God would reveal Himself, or he would have nothing to do with Him. *That* night, Aref watched Mohabat TV and prayed with the counselors for salvation. "I am in love with Jesus," he claimed!

203: Amir got saved a few months ago through Mohabat TV. He was only eleven years old. He heard about it through his dad who accepted Christ through Mohabat TV two years prior. One night Amir had a dream. He saw the city where he lived attacked by demonic spirits and saw a lake of blood. He fled by swimming and saw an island with a cross. A man offered his help and stretched his hand toward Amir. He said, "Give me your hand my child." Amir woke up and *knew* that man was Jesus!

204: Mostafa called Mohabat TV to share about his dream. He had a dream where Jesus loved him and said four words in English. He called the counselors to ask what his dream meant. They explained the Gospel, and the Lord *touched*

Mostafa's heart to accepted Jesus.

205: Mohammad called Mohabat TV from Tehran, Iran, to say that Jesus healed him when he was sleeping. He had chronic back pain for many years. Jesus Christ came to him while he slept, talked to him and said, "Stand up and walk. You are healed." When Mohammad woke up, he was *walking*.

206: Fariba called Mohabat TV from Northern Iran. She saw Jesus in a dream. She woke up and started looking for a Christian channel. Fariba found Mohabat TV and called the counselors to ask them many questions about Jesus. Then she prayed to *receive* Christ as her Lord and Savior.

207: Afsoon called to receive Christ. She was touched by a testimony shown on Mohabat TV. While praying for salvation, she saw a vision of angels standing around a hill. On the top of the hill was Jesus with a dove hovering around. Afsoon started crying and was filled with an *unspeakable* peace. She thanked the counselors so much for the programs.

208: Siamak gave his heart to the Lord six months ago while watching Mohabat TV, but he wasn't free from his drug addiction. Siamak prayed, and one night Jesus visited him. He touched his mind, and he was completely healed. Siamak was a new person! He didn't even know Jesus could heal his physical body and didn't think to pray about it. The next day, the pain in his feet went away, and he was completely healed. Siamak said he is also free from all his sexual thoughts. He said that God's *miracles* in his life never stop.

209: Zahra called Mohabat TV from Mashhad, Texas, to ask for a Bible. She watched the shows and was so interested that she went to bookstores looking for a Bible. One bookstore manager told her to come back, and he would find one for her. She left and decided not to go back. That night she had a vision of Jesus saying, "I am the bread of life. Follow me."

She called the counselors and prayed to receive Christ.

210: Azam had a dream that Jesus was calling her to follow him. She was very religious and ignored the dream. The next day, she saw Mohabat TV for the first time and started watching. While watching, Azam heard an audible voice behind her. "I am Jesus, follow me." She turned and saw no one! She resisted the urge to know Jesus and tried not to watch Mohabat again. A few days later, she had a dream again. Jesus said "Don't be afraid and walk with me on the water." Azam took his hand and *walked* with Jesus on the water. The next morning, she turned on Mohabat TV to see *The Jesus Film*, and when she saw Jesus walking on water with Peter, she wept and confessed Jesus is Lord.

211: Ahmad loves it when the counselors at Mohabat TV call him to explain the Bible to him. He said that he lost his right leg in an accident. He doesn't have any money. When he was in the hospital, he said he met Jesus and Mary in his hospital bed. He dreamed that Jesus invited him, took his hands and told him He would give him peace and health. A few days later, his roommates asked if he would like a good book. Amir said he started to read this book, and he's still reading it because it changed his life. Jesus speaks with him through this book. "I *love* Jesus," Ahmad said. He doesn't have any contact with Christians, church, Internet or computer. The counselors promised to call him every week to answer any questions and help him grow in his walk with God.

212: Mr. Bakhtiari was a devout Muslim. He watched Mohabat TV and called to argue. The counselors explained Christianity and that Jesus was the only way. He was not convinced, and the counselors prayed for him. That night, Mr. Bakhtiari had a dream that he was in a hospital full of Muslims who were worried, in pain and chaos. Then he saw himself in a Christian graveyard where all of the Christians were happy and peaceful! A man came to him and anointed his head with oil. The man asked him to believe in Him. When he woke up, he was confused and refused to believe in the dream. After days of frustration, Mr. Bakhtiari called with more questions and prayed to receive Christ. He asked prayer for his wife to get pregnant after seventeen years of no children. A month later he called happy that his wife was *pregnant*. He confessed that Jesus is the Son of God!

213: Mohammad called Mohabat TV from Kurdestan, Iran. He wanted to know what the programs were about. The counselors explained the Gospel and salvation. Mohammad prayed to receive Christ. That same night, he had a *dream* that Jesus was blessing him. He was so happy that he had found Jesus. He called the next day to express how happy he was and how much joy and happiness Jesus gave him and his family.

214: Sahar only knew Jesus as a prophet. After watching Mohabat TV, she was confronted with the fact that Jesus is the Son of God. She was confused. Days later, her friend who had received Jesus through the same program witnessed to her. Sahar prayed that Jesus would reveal His true self to her, and He did! He revealed himself through a vision and said, "I am." Sahar knew then for sure that He is *God*. She called the counselors to give her testimony.

215: Fereshteh called months earlier during a Mohabat TV prayer program to ask the counselors to pray for her husband. He was always angry. They prayed, and she testified that he changed so much and now wants to accept Jesus. She said after they prayed, her family saw a vision. While Fereshteh was sleeping, her family saw a powerful light over her that lit the room while she was sleeping. They were afraid and woke her up. As soon as Fereshteh woke up, the light left. She had a dream where she felt Jesus *loving* her and asking her to take care of her family. Now, all her family members have accepted Jesus Christ as their Lord.

216: Bayan, a lady from a small village in Iran, called Mohabat TV to ask the counselors why they claim that Jesus is Lord. She said every time she watched Mohabat TV, she got angry and cursed at the hosts. They explained the Gospel, and Bayan said bad things about Jesus and hung up. That night, she had a dream that Jesus explained He was Son of God. He put His hand over her head and said the repentance prayer. Bayan repeated after Him and accepted Jesus as her Lord and Savior. She called us to testify that she, including all her family, gave their life to Jesus!

217: Saeed, an Islamic scholar, had a dream of Jesus. He watched Mohabat TV and called to share that Jesus appeared to him and said, "The Father has sent me." Since then, Saeed said he experienced a tremendous joy. Jesus told him he needs to share this news with others. Saeed discussed this vision with a Mullah, and that Muslim clergy said all would be returned to Jesus! Saeed accepted Jesus as his Lord and Savior. He asked if the counselors knew other believers around him so that he could be *obedient* to Jesus and do what He asked him to do!

218: A woman saw doctors in Iran and Europe for a female problem she had since she was a teenager. She was unable to bear children. One night, the woman had a strange dream. She told one of the counselors about her dream, and the counselor prayed for her to receive healing. The woman called two years later to say her daughter, Arezou, which means *wish* or *hope* in Farsi, is nineteen months old now. She testified to the miracle and gave glory to God!

219: Hossein, an Afghan, called Mohabat TV from Iran. He got saved a few months ago. Two of his six sons were in prison in Iran. He called the counselors to pray for their release. They were all under surveillance from the Iranian government as a result of him leading his entire family to Christ after his salvation. Hossein didn't have the Bible yet and couldn't receive it due to his circumstances. The counselors later spoke to Hossein's daughter-in-law, who gave her heart to Jesus through a dream. In that dream, the Lord showed her that her husband, who was in jail at that time, would be released. The following day, her husband was free from prison. The Lord *delivered* her husband from drugs, and he told the counselor that he didn't want to touch them any longer. The desire for drugs left him, even after being addicted for the past eight years. Hossein's other son was also released from prison!

220: A woman watched Mohabat TV for a while and thought about this Jesus whom she knew. She thought he was a "prophet," because that's what she had learned growing up. This woman is a professor and teaches mathematics. Everything is logic to her. Recently, she began to have dreams. In one of her dreams, the woman saw an entire city filled with smoke, destruction and earthquakes. She was afraid, but she suddenly started to depart from the earth. She saw a young man asking for help. She helped that man by "flying" him over to her. They descended on a rooftop, and she saw the cross over the rooftop. She realized it was the roof of a church. While watching Mohabat TV, the woman called and shared her dreams. The counselors explained it was another golden opportunity to lead her to the Lord. They said the Lord was showing her calling as well, to bring others to Christ. The woman called back and asked the counselors to help her daughter to the Lord.

221: Mahmood watched Mohabat TV, and was encouraged to hear about the story in the Bible of the woman who was healed of her decade-long bleeding problem. That same night, he prayed to Jesus and said, "Lord if you are God and healed that women with the bleeding problem, heal my wife's back pain." The next morning, Mahmood's wife explained that she had a dream of Jesus coming to her and saying, "Let me heal you." Jesus started massaging her back and, when finished,

He said, "You are healed." Mahmood's wife was completely *healed* of her disk pain and could go around the house to do her chores. He called the counselors to explain the miracle and become a Christian.

222: Kamal called Mohabat TV and wanted to accept Jesus. He saw Jesus in a dream. Jesus gave him bread and water. When he woke up, Kamal *knew* that Jesus had changed him completely. He was so happy.

223: Ewaz, an Afghan, called Mohabat TV from Sweden. He said he was only *sixteen* years old. He shared his story with the counselors. "My father and my brother used to watch your TV program in Afghanistan. They both trusted Jesus. I trusted Jesus as a young boy in Afghanistan. But I did not understand much. The Taliban killed my father and my brother. I was young, and my mother helped me get out of Afghanistan to Iran. I was bitter in my life because of what happened to my father and my brother. With a lot of difficulty, I reached Sweden. Here in Sweden I did not want to do anything with God or religion. I was lonely. One night I was dreaming that I was caught in a storm in the middle of ocean. There were a lot of people in the boat, and the boat was drowning, and it was dark. At this time, I saw a man who said, 'Take my hand. I am your Savior.' I am thankful to God for saving my life. Soon after that, I met with some of my own Hazara people in Sweden who helped me understand more about Jesus. I praise God that since I am in the fellowship of God's people, He has healed me and has changed my life. I am thankful to Him."

7: THE PURSUIT OF PEACE AND JOY

"Blessed are the *peacemakers*: for they shall be called sons of God" (Matthew 5:9, emphasis added).

224: Seven Afghan friends liked watching Mohabat TV together. One day, they called to confess they know that Islam is not from God. They asked the counselors many questions, and all accepted Jesus as their Lord. They were filled with peace and joy, *and* all of them were so happy!

225: Kimya called Mohabat TV from Thailand. She said she always watches the programs but had never prayed to receive Christ. Kimya said she never thought she would become a Christian. The counselors explained what it means to be a Christian, and she joyfully accepted Jesus. She said she feels so alone in Thailand and doesn't know anyone, but she is happy that she found the *true* joy of her life.

226: Mohsen, a fifty-five-year-old man, called Mohabat TV to ask what the channel was about. The counselors explained and told him about Christ and salvation. Mohsen loved what he heard. He said he had never called a channel before. He always watched, but this was the first time he called while watching Mohabat TV. Mohsen was so fed up with his life. His wife and kids had left him, and he lived alone. He had a good living, owned a factory and had many workers. Mohsen said he always felt alone. He now knows that he is not alone, *and* someone cares for him. Mohsen was filled with peace and joy when he prayed to receive Christ. He started to cry and said, "It's such a good feeling. I want it to stay."

227: A Muslim Persian lady called Mohabat TV from Iraq. She had no one and felt very alone. She needed to talk with someone but told the counselors not to talk about religion. In spite of her refusing to talk about God, they told her that Jesus could give her peace. When they called to follow up with the Persian lady, she said she tested God, *and* He gave her a peace she'd never experienced before. She was full of joy!

228: Leyla called Mohabat TV from Yazd, Iran, to ask for prayer. She was sick of her life and sleeping with other men. When the counselors talked with her about Jesus, she cried and accepted the Lord. After they hung up, she called back five minutes later to say she felt so relieved. Leyla said, "This joy is too good, *and* I will never go back to my old life!"

229: A man heard a guy in the park talking about Jesus on the phone. He listened and asked this man who he was talking to, and if he could know Jesus, too. He got Mohabat TV's number and called our counselors to say he had stopped praying in Islam. He was just praying to God and now he wanted to know who this Jesus was. The counselors explained how to give his heart to the Lord. The man claimed he found the truth, *and* he's never been this happy before!

230: Maryam called Mohabat TV to ask for prayer from Iran. Her family was all Christian except for her. The counselors told her to trust in the Lord and open her heart to Him. Maryam did and prayed for salvation. In the middle of her prayer, she started crying and said her body felt very hot. She called back ten minutes later to say there was a special odor in her house. She said it smelled like incense *and* was so comforting. Mary said, "I know it is God's presence!" She said joy entered her house., and the next day she gave her testimony on the air during a live program.

231: Naser called Mohabat TV from Tabriz, Iran, wondering what the programs were all about. The counselors explained that they talked about Jesus, the Son of God. Naser argued sharply and hung up. He called back to ask many questions, wanting them to explain more. Naser said he needed to talk to his wife and would call them back. The next day, he called with such joy *and* prayed to receive Jesus!

232: Fatemeh called Mohabat TV thinking it was another TV show. When she realized it was a Christian show, Fatemeh was shocked. She never watches or has anything to do with religious programs. The counselors said that it wasn't an accident that she called. They witnessed to her, *and* she accepted Jesus. She was so full of joy that her family prayed to accept Jesus, too!

233: Mohammad watched Mohabat TV and was surprised to hear why the Islamic religion was wrong. He called and asked so many questions. Finally, Mohammad believed Jesus is the only answer. He prayed for salvation *and* called back later to say how happy he is. His whole life has changed since he watched Mohabat TV!

234: Kazem called Mohabat TV from Iran while sobbing. He was so sad because his wife left him and took his two daughters. He said he had only seen them once in two weeks. Every time the counselors tried to talk to him, he broke into tears and hung up the phone. Finally, they got Kazem to listen to the message of the Gospel, *and* he prayed to receive Jesus as his Lord. He felt so light and joyful. He was laughing when he hung up!

235: While Alireza was watching Mohabat TV, God's presence fell all over him. His wife had left him and took their son. He felt so depressed and hated his messed up life. Alireza prayed with the counselors *and* was filled with joy. Jesus embraced him with His peace.

236: Soosan called Mohabat TV to testify that after she believed in Christ, her life changed completely. There is now peace in their home. Her family was able to buy a house and a car. Her husband is now free from drugs, *and* the money they lost from her husband's job is being returned to them. Soosan said, "Jesus blessed us with so much peace and joy."

237: Hamzeh was released from a mental hospital, and started watching Mohabat TV. He was depressed. He couldn't remember ever feeling joy and peace in his life. He used to go and beg on the streets. He called Mohabat TV to be prayed for. A week later, Hamzeh called back to say that God set him free from demons. He confessed that, for the first time in his life, "I'm happy!" He said he sleeps peacefully now. He can't wait to look for a job *and* meet new people, which he has never done before!

238: Soheila was very depressed and wanted to kill herself. She found Mohabat TV while she was yelling and questioning God. After watching, she called with many questions. The counselors explained how Jesus died so she could have life. She prayed to accept Christ. Soheila was suddenly filled with joy *and* peace. She said, "I feel I am born again."

239: Azadeh prayed to receive Christ with the counselors at Mohabat TV. She called three days later to share her thoughts and feelings and how they had changed. Azadeh said she used to be anxious and worried about everything, but, since she prayed, she felt a peace and joy of God all over her. She said, "Jesus changed my life, *and* already my family is noticing that!"

240: Ali received a tape from his friend, who always recorded Mohabat TV to pass along to his friends. Ali said he always felt heavy, and a bad spirit bothered him. When he watched, he prayed, "If Jesus is Lord, you can free me." Immediately, the room was filled with God's presence, *and* Ali was set free!

He felt so light and happy that he called the counselors rejoicing to give his testimony.

241: Hossein called Mohabat TV from Iran to curse and say bad words to the counselors. He continued harassing and called with questions about Islam. One day, Hossein watched how people called during a live show to say how God had answered their prayers. He called and asked for prayer for his ex-wife to return. He was very depressed after she left him. The counselors continued to speak to him about Jesus and salvation. Hossein said he would think about it and call back. Two days later, he called to say he felt peace. He wanted to accept Jesus. Hossein was happy to become a Christian. He said, "I would never imagine I would accept Jesus as the son of God. But He is real, and has given me peace and joy." He called back again one week later to testify on air how Jesus changed him. He said, "I used to make fun and curse at Christians, and now I am one of them! I cannot even sin now." Hossein said when his wife left him, he used to sleep with other women. But when a friend came over to his house, he couldn't sleep with her. Hossein said it didn't feel right, *and* he could not sin!

242: Leyla was in her twenties. For years she dealt with a spirit of fear and depression. She was afraid of everything, including death, and couldn't stay overnight at her parents' house or travel to see her brother and sister because of fear. One night, she laid down and watched Mohabat TV. She called the counselors to be delivered from all these spirits. Her husband wasn't home when she called, but he had gotten her a satellite on loan to "maybe" help her. For years, Leyla spent money on witches to be free and obviously got worse. After Leyla prayed for salvation, she was filled with joy *and* peace. While in tears, she thanked Jesus for this new hope in her heart.

243: A woman called Mohabat TV while on drugs. She sounded suicidal. The counselors felt she had a spirit of death upon her. They answered her questions and bound the spirit of death on her life. The woman said her parents were heavily involved with witchcraft as it was their jobs. She had many witches' items and "their prayers" in her room. She couldn't sleep due to nightmares. After she prayed for salvation, she said how she suddenly felt peaceful *and* joyful. She decided to burn her witches' items and prayers and move in with her sister in another town.

244: Ayatollah, an young Afghan man, called Mohabat TV from Holland. He wanted to become a Christian but was afraid. He said, "I love your programs and love your God. But there is a fear in me that is not allowing me to become a Christian! What should I do?" The counselors explained that religion brings fear, but Jesus Christ brings you peace with God that no religion can give. When they preached the Gospel, he started crying and prayed for salvation. Ayatollah was so relieved, but his crying would not stop. He explained he never cries, *and* that he is so happy. He said, "I am crying tears of joy!"

245: Arash's friend witnessed to him about Jesus. He was already a believer, but he saw a true peace and joy in his friend's life. He called Mohabat TV to rededicate his life to Jesus, *and* while they were praying, he cried. He said, "I feel the warmth of the Holy Spirit upon me."

246: Rahele, a seventeen-year-old, accidentally changed channels and found Mohabat TV. She watched it a few times and suddenly found the peace and joy she was missing. Rahele waited a week to call to give her testimony *and* heart to Jesus on the air!

247: A man called Mohabat TV from Dushanbe, Tajikistan. He said, "I just wanted to call and say that I started watching your shows. It has been three months since I committed my life to Christ. I called to give this good news. I am a trader by profession, and I have seen God's *miracles* in my life after watching your shows."

248: K called Mohabat TV from Qom, Iran, to ask about Jesus. After talking with the counselors, he still wasn't convinced. A few weeks later, K emailed to say he now *knows* Jesus is God. He wrote that one morning he was confused while thinking about who God is. Suddenly, he said, his mind just lit up. He doesn't know "how" he knew, but he all of a sudden joyfully understood the truth.

249: Abbass called Mohabat TV from Bushehr, Iran. He had questions about the book of Revelation and the end times. He was a student at Islam University and had many questions about his school project. The counselors answered his questions, and he was surprised by their answers. After the long phone call, Abbass *accepted* Jesus as his Savior with *joy*!

250: Abbas called Mohabat TV from Iran to say he had been watching for a few months. He wanted to know more about Christianity. He prayed the salvation prayer with the host during a live program and sobbed that he had found *joy* in the true God!

251: Saeed, an Afghan, called Mohabat TV from Afghanistan. He watched many times before he called in for prayer. Saeed said he couldn't stop crying. After he prayed the salvation prayer with the counselors, he said he felt a *joy* he had never experienced before!

252: Hussain, an Afghan, called Mohabat TV to express his love for Jesus. He was unaware that he could become a Christian. When the counselors explained the Gospel, he prayed to receive Christ. Hussain was filled with such joy that it actually surprised him. He felt so good that he called ten of his friends, *and* they all prayed to accept Jesus as their Lord and Savior. Hussain said, "We are all Afghans, and this joy and peace is impossible for us. But Jesus loves us so much that He called us to His Kingdom!"

8: FORBIDDEN FAITH

"Blessed are they that have been *persecuted* for righteousness' sake: for theirs is the kingdom of heaven. Blessed are ye when men shall *reproach* you, and *persecute* you, and say all manner of evil against you falsely, for my sake" (Matthew 5:10-11, emphasis added).

253: Nasrin was given a Bible in the airport, but never read it or believed in Christ. She took it back with her into Iran, and the authorities arrested her after they found it in customs. Nasrin said she was taken to an unknown private garden and raped multiple times by different men. After many days of torture, she escaped. Nasrin said her friend who was a believer in Christ took her in. While she was recovering, she watched Mohabat TV and called to ask for prayer. Nasrin argued with the counselors and questioned God. She said, "Why did He allow this to happen?" After many phone calls, Nasrin prayed to receive Christ. She told the counselors she couldn't go back home to see her fifteen-year-old son for fear of the authorities. Her brother eventually helped her escape to Turkey with her son. While they were fleeing, the Islamic services ran over Nasrin's brother with a truck and killed him instantly. He was only twenty four years old, and two weeks away from his wedding. Nasrin said when she *found* Jesus, she lost everything!

254: Maryam called Mohabat TV from Kermanshah, Iran. She said she has invited many people, including relatives, into her home to watch Mohabat TV. So far, because of her, more than *forty* people have given their hearts to Jesus.

255: Bahram called Mohabat TV to ask questions about Jesus. He wanted to accept Jesus in his heart, but was afraid of his family because they were Muslim. The counselors explained Christianity to Bahram, who started shaking. He said he couldn't hold the phone. Bahram called back a few minutes later, and said he couldn't stop crying! He said he felt God's presence and *immediately* prayed the salvation prayer with the counselors!

256: Hamid, a young Afghan, called Mohabat TV to say he had lost everything since becoming a Christian. His parents threw him out of the house because they claimed he was now unclean. He said he also lost his job, friends and family. Hamid said he counted it as joy for the Lord even when his father died, and he wasn't allowed to go to the funeral. Hamid cried and said, "It's all worth it. I will *never* let go of Jesus!"

257: Siavash called Mohabat TV to ask for prayer. He said he fled to Turkey from Iran because he was in danger since becoming a Christian five years ago. He said during the elections, he felt led to arrange with local doctors and nurses to treat the injured in homes he had previously arranged. He had no idea the elections led to so many injuries. Siavash said he was able to help many avoid the hospital. He said, "Once you go to the hospital they will take you to prison, and you never know what happens after that." He said he saved *many* lives. Even though God used him mightily, he still had to flee Iran because the authorities were searching to kill him. He asked for prayer for a new life in Turkey.

258: An Afghan man living in Iran called Mohabat TV to talk about Jesus. He asked for prayer and said, "I am tired of Islam and all its deceit. I want to know the truth." The man said he and his family had to leave Afghanistan. The counselors prayed, and he accepted the Lord with joy. He thanked them for praying for his family who had lost everything.

259: An Afghan man called Mohabat TV from Sweden asking for prayer. He said he became a Christian while watching the programs. The man said his wife and kids left him because he became a Christian. He also had to run from his country. He said while he was in Austria at a Persian church, he asked to be baptized. On the day of his baptism, his cousin threw boiling water on him. The man said he had to go to the emergency room for his burns after getting baptized. He said, "Everyone in my family is against me. I *only* have Jesus."

260: Arezoo called Mohabat TV from Afghanistan. She said her family had watched for some time and had many questions about Christianity. The counselors answered their questions and explained the Gospel. Arezoo's whole family of *ten* gave their lives to Christ.

261: Ali was so impacted by watching the testimonies on Mohabat TV that he called to find out if they were all true. The counselors answered his many questions, and Ali prayed to received Jesus. Two days later, Ali called back to say his Muslim family kicked him out of the house because they were upset with him. He said his friend let him stay at his house because he was afraid to be seen by his relatives. He said, "I will stand for Jesus to the end."

262: Novin watched both the Islamic channel and Mohabat TV. He called to ask questions about Islam and Christianity. One day, he called and said, "I came to this conclusion that Christians say the *truth*, and the Mullahs are wrong." He prayed to receive Jesus with the counselors.

263: Nasrin called Mohabat TV from Borujerd, Iran. She thanked them and said she now knows that Islam is a false religion. Nasrin said she was a very devout Muslim woman. She did everything she could to please God, but she never felt satisfied or fulfilled in her religious duties. She said, "Thank you for *opening* my eyes to the truth." She prayed the salvation prayer during a live show on air with the host.

264: Kourosh was studying to be a Mullah. One day he was flipping channels and came across Mohabat TV. He said he was so impacted by the testimonies on the live show that he called in to ask questions. Kourosh said everything became so clear for him, and he, along with *three* of his friends, prayed for salvation with the counselors!

265: Iraj was a theology student in Iran. He called Mohabat TV to say: "I am studying Islam, but I know it is not the truth. I always pray to God to show me the truth. I came across your channel, and I want to know the true God." The counselors explained to him the Good News of the Gospel. Iraj prayed to receive Christ and was so *relieved* to finally know the truth.

266: Aziz called Mohabat TV from Afghanistan to say Christians were being attacked and jailed. He wanted to know more about *this* Jesus. He prayed the prayer of salvation with the counselors. In spite of recent persecution, Aziz brought eleven of his friends to faith because of the transformation Jesus did in his life through Mohabat TV.

267: Hava, an older lady from Iran, was registered to go to Mecca and become a Hadji. Her daughter had recently become a Christian and told her about Jesus. Hava called Mohabat TV to learn more about the Jesus who changed her daughter so much. After understanding the Good News, Hava accepted Jesus and *cancelled* her trip to Mecca!

268: Zahra was at a friend's house in Shiraz, Iran, when they watched Mohabat TV. Her friend told her about Jesus, and they called the counselors for prayer. Zahra became a Christian that day because of the *boldness* of her friend!

269: Parviz called Mohabat TV to learn more about Jesus and Christianity. He said that he owned a satellite for years but never watched the channel. After he found it, Parviz listened to the other Muslims who called in to argue. He said he was impressed by the compassion of the counselors toward all of them. He was *happy* to give his heart to the Lord over the phone!

270: Heydar called Mohabat TV to give his heart to Jesus. He told the counselors he is an uneducated villager and a shepherd. He said he doesn't have much, but he can't stop witnessing to everyone he meets to tell them about Jesus. Even though it's dangerous to be a Christian where he lives, Heydar continues to tell *everyone* about Jesus.

271: Mohsen had already been a student at the Islamic school of Qom for seven years when he called Mohabat TV. He spent most of his time studying Islam and searching for the truth. Mohsen called the counselors because he had many questions about Christianity. The counselors listened and answered *all* of his questions. Mohsen said, "I am so happy I found the truth." He then prayed to receive Jesus as his Lord and Savior.

272: Ali, an Iranian, was visiting Turkey when he called Mohabat TV for a church address in Istanbul. The counselors connected him with a local church. While Ali was there, he gave his life to Jesus. His family noticed the *change* in him when he returned. Ali called back to say that his wife and children also prayed to give their lives to Jesus.

273: Marzieh's husband accepted Jesus in Sweden. He came back to Iran and told his wife about Jesus. After she watched *The Jesus Film* on Mohabat TV, she accepted Christ, along with their two kids. They started a house *church* using Mohabat TV's programs to reach Muslims in their area and to grow in their faith.

274: Vahid called Mohabat TV from Afghanistan. He called to argue with the counselors that Jesus was only a prophet. After a year of calling to argue, he called back. Instead of arguing with the counselors, he listened to them. Vahid prayed to receive Jesus as His Lord and Savior because he was *impacted* by the Mohabat TV programs and the words of Jesus.

275: Ali called Mohabat TV from Saudi Arabia. He said even though his family was against Christianity, he loved Jesus. Ali asked them how he could become a Christian and accept Jesus in his *heart*.

276: Fereshteh called Mohabat TV from Iran. She cried while the counselors prayed for her. She said her family was against Christianity and that they were always fighting with each other. She called back after she prayed for salvation to say she is now at complete *peace* despite the turmoil in her home.

277: Mohsen called Mohabat TV from Syria. He confessed that the programs open his eyes to the truth, and he wanted to accept Jesus along with his wife. They prayed with the counselors and said, "We now understand that Islam is a *false* religion."

278: Hamideh's friend told her about Mohabat TV. She became a Christian and told her husband that she didn't want to go to Mecca with him. Hamideh's husband insisted, and she called for prayer for their trip. After she got back, she called to say that God blessed their trip, and she was able to *witness* to people while she was there.

279: A woman called Mohabat TV from Qom, Iran. She told the counselors that she was raped by her boyfriend. She needed an operation and was hiding in her friend's house for fear her family was going to kill her. The counselors prayed for her and told her about the love of Jesus. The woman not only accepted Jesus, but *witnessed* to her friend about her newfound joy in the Lord!

280: Khodadad called Mohabat TV from Bojnord, Iran, to ask how he could become a Christian. The counselors shared with him how he could pray to receive Christ. A few days later, Khodadad called back to introduce his friends and neighbors to Mohabat TV. They all wanted to become Christians! Khodadad was so on fire for the Lord that he shared the Good News of the Gospel with everyone. He invited each person he met back to his home and welcomed them to watch Mohabat TV. He called every few days with new families who also wanted to become Christians, and receive Bibles. So far, the counselors believe more than *two hundred* people have become Christians because of Khodadad!

281: Behzad called Mohabat TV from Tajikistan. He said, "I called to let you know that I have been watching your programs, and now I am a Christian. I love the Lord because He changed my life. I always pray for Mohabat TV. When someone gives their testimony on a live program, I weep for joy. Praise be to Jesus who is going to *change* the people of Tajikistan, Iran and Afghanistan soon!"

282: Reza called Mohabat TV to ask if the counselors could speak to his friend who needed prayer. He said, "I am a Pashtun, and I have lived a very hard life. I have seen and experienced the bitterness of life. Many years ago, I found Mohabat TV when I was living in Greece. This was the first time I ever heard about Jesus. I literally felt like He was the only medication I ever needed for healing. After I moved, I continued to watch even though I was rejected by my family members, including my brothers. If I am beaten, spit upon or even killed, I have *no* regrets because I now have Jesus."

283: Ali, an Afghan living in Germany, called Mohabat TV to share his story. He said, "I so badly wanted to share my testimony, but, as you know, life in Europe is hard. By the time I come home from work, your shows are over. Today I ran to reach the end of the live show. I want you to know that I used to be a godless person. I was depressed and hopeless. I never saw Afghanistan because my parents were refugees in Iran where I was born. I thought all religions were the same until I went to church in Germany. Even though I didn't speak the language, I was welcomed with grace. Their love made all of the *difference*. This is how God saved me!"

284: Najib, an Afghan living in Sweden, called Mohabat TV to share his story. He said, "I am from Ningarhar, Afghanistan. I was in the Afghan army, where I met a foreigner who told me about Jesus. I argued with him about Christianity, but he never told me I was wrong. He humbly gave me *The Jesus Film*, and asked me to watch it. After I watched the film, everything changed. I became a follower of Jesus and had to flee to Europe. It was there I *found* other Afghan and Iranian Christians!"

285: Salim, an Afghan living in Sweden, called Mohabat TV. He said, "I am an Afghan, and all my life I knew there was an emptiness in my life. My soul craved for peace, freedom and truth. I searched in Islam and could not find the peace I longed for. God brought me to Sweden, and I lived with an Iranian who already trusted Jesus. He used to read his Bible, but I ignored him. One day when he wasn't home, I started reading the Bible. That was it for me! I loved reading the Bible and started going to church. Every question I had was answered in grace. Their loving behavior *impacted* my life so much."

286: Zia, an Afghan living in Sweden, called Mohabat TV to share his story. He said, "I am from Afghanistan. I recently heard the Good News of the Gospel for the first time. I believe God touched my life. I have no other reason to come on the live show other than to give my *testimony!*"

287: An Afghan family living in Europe called during a Mohabat TV live show to share their story. The husband shared, "I didn't want to come on your live show because I didn't want to get my family members still living in Afghanistan in trouble. I know there are many things I will never understand, but I want to thank the counselors for answering all my questions over the past few years. My wife and our two children are now *ready* to become Christians!"

288: Reza called Mohabat TV from Tehran, Iran. He had questions about Christianity. He asked the counselors if there was an office he could go to in Tehran to ask questions about Jesus. The counselors explained a safe way to exchange email or call them with any questions. After several email exchanges, Reza called to *receive* Christ over the phone!

289: A sixteen-year-old called Mohabat TV to share his story. He said, "My mother is Iranian, and my father is an Afghan. I hated your channel, and every time I watched I got so angry. A few weeks ago, I started to listen more. I felt God's peace. I now know that Jesus is the only way. I want to accept Jesus as my Savior, and I know there will be consequences with my family, but I am *ready*!"

290: A couple called Mohabat TV twelve days after they became Christians. They asked the counselors to pray for the husband who was fired from his job after they found out he was a Christian. They only gave him three days to find a new job. The wife was sad, but the husband told her not to worry. They prayed, and the couple called back a few days later to thank them for the prayers! The husband found a *new* job!

291: Mahmoud was a student of the Islamic school in Qom. He called during Ramadan to ask about fasting. The counselors explained that salvation is through grace alone and not by works, which includes fasting. Mahmoud prayed to receive Christ with the counselors.

292: Pejhman called Mohabat TV from Dezful, Iran, to say the shows were very boring! He said he found the station when he was flipping channels. He told the counselors that he doesn't believe in God. He said they were wasting their time talking about God. At first, Pejhman argued with the counselors, but the more he realized they were answering all of his questions, the more he gave in. He said his heart felt lighter after they prayed.

293: Fahimeh called Mohabat TV to share how lonely she was. She said, "I don't have anybody. I am a hard-working mother, but I have no money. I was thirty years old when I became a widow. I watch your programs and pray daily. I take notes and share with the rest of my family what I hear. Now, I am experiencing peace. Even my daughter-in-law purchased a cross necklace, and my mother got interested in this, too. I am fifty-four years old now and still am worried about the future of my children." Fahimeh prayed to receive Christ with the counselors. She broke into tears and said, "I am such a sinner. Do you think Jesus will *accept* me?" The counselors told her there was no need to wash herself. Jesus already accept her just as she was. After Fahimeh prayed, she said, "I feel light as a feather!"

294: Omid called Mohabat TV with a friend to ask theological questions. He was studying Islamic studies and wanted to become a Mullah. The counselors shared Christianity with Omid and his friend. They said they wanted to accept Jesus in their hearts but were afraid they couldn't tell their parents because they were Muslim. They did anyway, and after accepting Jesus said they felt peaceful. They said if they are asked to leave their parents house, they are no longer *afraid* because they have Jesus!

295: Saeed and twenty of his friends at the university watched Mohabat TV regularly. He called to ask how they could become Christians and start a house church. The counselors led *all* twenty plus students to pray and receive Christ as their Lord. Then they explained how they could worship together and start a house church!

296: Rahmat, an Afghan living in Sweden, called Mohabat TV. He said, "I am thankful that I am a Christian. God used Afghans in my life, including Mohabat TV, to help me understand the depth of God's grace and love. I used to think it was a great sin to enter into a church until I needed help. I found the grace of God through the worshipers even though I didn't speak the language. God used many different ways to make Himself known to me, and because of that, I *share* Jesus wherever I go!"

297: Omid was a graduate from the Islamic Theological University in Qom. He watched Mohabat to study and better understand Christianity. He called the counselors to ask more questions. When he heard more about Christianity, Omid was shocked. He expressed his disappointment in Islam and said, "They lied to us and deceived us to be Muslim." Omid *prayed* to receive Christ. His wife was a theological student and did not want to accept Christ, but she allowed the counselors to pray for her!

298: Ebrahim called Mohabat TV from Esfahan, Iran. He had called and asked questions without introducing himself. Finally, he called back and confessed: "I am the one who was asking all those Bible questions. Now I am ready to give my life to Jesus!" When Ebrahim called, there were about ten friends listening on the speaker phone. The counselors answered all of their questions about Jesus. During the salvation prayer, one of the ten fell to the ground and said, "I feel God's *power* on me, and I have goose bumps!"

299: Mehdi called Mohabat TV from Iran to pray to receive Christ with the counselors. Two weeks later, he called back and asked them to speak to some of his friends who had recently been to Mecca in Saudi Arabia. The counselors asked Mehdi to put them on speaker phone, and after explaining the Good News of the Gospel, they all prayed to receive Christ. Mehdi threw a party for his friends who prayed and asked the counselors how he could start an "underground church." The second time Mehdi called, forty-five more people became Christians over speaker phone. The counselors said they heard lots of screaming and clapping! Mehdi said they had made a feast of fruits, sweets and cookies for those who became Christians. The third time Mehdi called the counselors to put them on speaker phone, a high ranking Islamic judge was there!

CONCLUSION

Now, more than ever, one is able to reach Iran with the Gospel of Christ through media (TV, websites, social media). This helps fulfill the mandate or call from the Bible to remember the persecuted church, "Remember the prisoners as if chained with them—those who are mistreated—since you yourselves are in the body also" (Hebrews 13:3, NKJV).

Here are four ways to get involved with Heart4Iran starting today!

Pray. Pray for the church. Pray for dreams and visions among Muslims. Pray for Muslims to have more encounters with Scripture. Pray for the unreached people of Iran.

Engage. There is a revival happening right now inside Iran. Learn more about Heart4Iran and its partner organizations on the website or by emailing us at engage@heart4iran.com.

Advocate. The UN reports that Iran has some of the highest rates of depression, drug abuse, suicide and prostitution in the region. To reach the hopeless in Iran, we must pray against the threats against God's people including: arrests, torture and even death. Iranians are eager for solutions to help their dissolving families, distressed faith communities and societal structures. We believe that change is on the horizon. It will take time, but it will happen. Join us by telling others about the needs of this critical nation and watch the change happen.

Support. We are confident that media resources provided through satellite television, Internet, mobile platforms and social networks continue to accomplish a tremendous work by pointing Muslims to Christ's message of love, encouraging new believers and supporting the efforts of the local church. Giving to the Heart4Iran network focusing on Iran is a great way to help reach this critical nation. Together we are better.

NOTES

1. *The paradox that is Persia*, accessed September 2, 2015, https://www.youtube.com/watch?v=k-y93AZhsBU.
2. *70% of Iran's Population is Under the Age of 35*, accessed September 1, 2015, http://hormozshariat.com/2013/09/10/5-things-you-didnt-know-about-iran-2/.
3. *The paradox that is Persia*, accessed September 2, 2015, https://www.youtube.com/watch?v=k-y93AZhsBU.
4. *Evangelical Growth*, accessed February 16, 2016, http://www.operationworld.org/hidden/evangelical-growth.

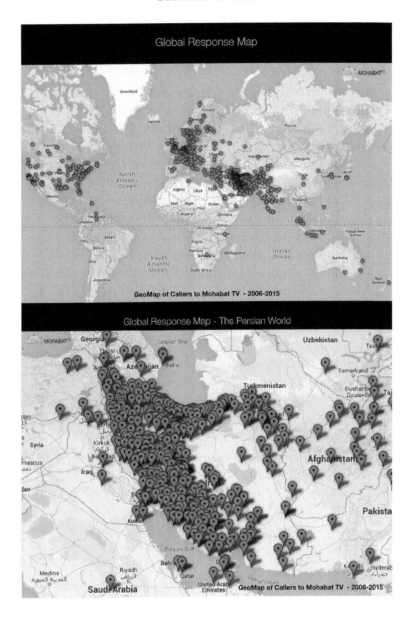

GeoMap of Callers to Mohabat TV - 2006-2015

GeoMap of Callers to Mohabat TV - 2006-2015

ABOUT THE AUTHOR

Dr. Mike Ansari is the President of Heart4Iran, a non-political partnership of multi-national organizations whose number one aim is to serve and bless the people of Iran.

Mike was born into a secular Muslim family in the city of Shiraz, Iran. At the age of seven he experienced the Iranian Islamic Revolution and witnessed the death of many Iranians, including his cousin. The events of his early life led him to question Islam, spirituality and God. Through a series of events, Mike came to the United States and dedicated himself to academics, becoming a biochemist and a doctor. His mother came to follow Jesus Christ through a dream. The change was so dramatic that Mike also gave his life to Jesus.

Early in his walk as a new Christian, God gave Mike a burden to bring unity to the church and help equip worshippers inside Iran, so he started FarsiPraise Ministries. Years later, he was asked to join Mohabat TV and help with its management and development. He serves as the director of operations for Mohabat TV and leads Heart4Iran. During his tenure, Mike has managed to successfully develop one of the largest and most successful models of partnership among dozens of ministries serving the Farsi speakers of Iran, Afghanistan and Tajikistan.

A gifted leader and speaker, Mike and his team are available to conduct TV and radio interviews and speak at churches, youth groups and ministry events.

Made in the USA
San Bernardino, CA
20 April 2018